More Games

▲▼▲▼▲▼▲▼▲▼▲ ▲▼▲▼▲▼▲▼▲

to Play With
Toddlers

▲▼▲▼▲▼▲▼▲▼▲▼▲▼▲▼▲▼▲▼▲▼▲▼▲▼▲▼▲▼▲▼▲▼▲

More Games to Play with Toddlers

■

Jackie Silberg

Illustrations by Cheryl Kirk Noll

gryphon house

Beltsville, Maryland

▲▼▲▼▲▼▲▼▲▼▲▼▲▼▲▼▲▼▲▼▲▼▲▼▲▼▲▼▲

Published by Gryphon House, Inc.
10726 Tucker Street, Beltsville MD 20705

World Wide Web: http://www.ghbooks.com

The author of this book, Jackie Silberg, is an acclaimed speaker, teacher and trainer on early childhood development and music. You can arrange to have her speak, present, train or entertain by contacting her through Gryphon House, PO Box 207, Beltsville MD 20704-0207.

Cover Design: Graves Fowler Associates
Cover Illustration: Cheryl Kirk Noll
Text Illustrations: Cheryl Kirk Noll

Library of Congress Cataloging-in-Publication Data

Silberg, Jackie, 1924-

    More games to play with toddlers / Jackie Silberg : illustrations by Cheryl Kirk Noll.
       p. cm.
      ISBN 0-87659-178-0 (pbk.)
      1. Games. 2. Educational games. 3. Toddlers. I. Title.
GV 1203. S5385   1996   98-15002
793'.01922--dc20   CIP

Table of Contents

▲▼▲▼▲▼▲▼▲▼▲▼▲▼▲▼▲▼▲▼▲▼▲▼▲▼▲▼▲

Block Games

▲▼▲▼▲▼▲▼▲▼▲▼▲▼▲▼▲▼▲▼▲▼▲▼▲▼▲▼▲▼▲▼▲▼▲▼▲▼

Bouncing Games

▲▼▲▼▲▼▲▼▲▼▲▼▲▼▲▼▲▼▲▼▲▼▲▼▲▼▲▼▲▼▲▼▲▼▲▼▲▼

▲▼▲▼▲▼▲▼▲▼▲▼▲▼▲▼▲▼▲▼▲▼▲▼▲▼▲▼▲

Color and Shape Games

▲▼

Language Games

▲▼

▲▼▲▼▲▼▲▼▲▼▲▼▲▼▲▼▲▼▲▼▲▼▲▼▲▼▲▼▲▼▲▼▲▼▲▼▲▼▲

Outside Games

▲▼

▲▼▲▼▲▼▲▼▲▼▲▼▲▼▲▼▲▼▲▼▲▼▲▼▲▼▲▼▲▼▲▼▲▼▲▼▲

Quiet Games

▲▼▲▼▲▼▲▼▲▼▲▼▲▼▲▼▲▼▲▼▲▼▲▼▲▼▲▼▲▼▲▼▲▼▲▼▲▼

Rhyming Games

▲▼▲▼▲▼▲▼▲▼▲▼▲▼▲▼▲▼▲▼▲▼▲▼▲▼▲▼▲▼▲▼▲▼▲▼▲▼

▲▼▲▼▲▼▲▼▲▼▲▼▲▼▲▼▲▼▲▼▲▼▲▼▲▼▲▼▲▼▲▼▲

Running and Jumping Games

▲▼▲▼▲▼▲▼▲▼▲▼▲▼▲▼▲▼▲▼▲▼▲▼▲▼▲▼▲▼▲▼▲▼▲▼

▲▼▲▼▲▼▲▼▲▼▲▼▲▼▲▼▲▼▲▼▲▼▲▼▲▼▲▼▲▼▲▼▲

Seasonal Games

▲▽▲▽▲▽▲▽▲▽▲▽▲▽▲▽▲▽▲▽▲▽▲▽▲▽▲▽▲▽▲▽▲▽▲▽

Singing Games

▲▽▲▽▲▽▲▽▲▽▲▽▲▽▲▽▲▽▲▽▲▽▲▽▲▽▲▽▲▽▲▽▲▽▲▽

Social Games

Toy Games

▲▼

▲▼▲▼▲▼▲▼▲▼▲▼▲▼▲▼▲▼▲▼▲▼▲▼▲▼▲▼▲▼▲▼▲

From the Author

▲▼▲▼▲▼▲▼▲▼▲▼▲▼▲▼▲▼▲▼▲▼▲▼▲▼▲▼▲▼▲

What is more precious than a toddler exploring the world, dropping food on the floor to see if it will bounce, running and hitting a wall over and over, listening to the same story or song hundreds of times! Toddlers learn from all of these experiences. Every day, when your child plays, she is developing listening, language, cognitive, motor, social and self-esteem skills that you as a parent and teacher want her to have.

This book is a continuation of *Games to Play With Toddlers* and contains fresh, innovative and stimulating games for you and your child to play and grow together. Whether it's building with blocks, whispering at quiet times, playing with toys or laughing together, you will find lots of terrific ideas to enjoy with your child and help her learn.

What could be more memorable than opening up your arms wide and having that darling toddler run into them with an enormous hug and a big, wet kiss!

Enjoy!

Jackie Silberg

Jackie Silberg

▲▼▲▼▲▼▲▼▲▼▲▼▲▼▲▼▲▼▲▼▲▼▲▼▲▼▲▼▲▼▲

Guidelines for Growth

▲▽▲▽▲▽▲▽▲▽▲▽▲▽▲▽▲▽▲▽▲▽▲▽▲▽▲▽▲

Motor, Auditory and Visual Skills
▲▽▲▽▲▽▲▽▲▽▲▽▲▽▲▽▲▽▲▽▲▽▲▽▲▽▲▽▲▽▲▽▲▽▲▽▲▽

Walks independently

Walks up and down stairs holding an adult's hand

Holds two small objects in one hand

Jumps in place

Kicks a large ball

Throws a small ball overhand

Recognizes familiar people

Scribbles on paper

Stacks three to six blocks

Turns knobs

Finds objects of the same color, shape and size

Points to distant, interesting objects outdoors

Turns toward a family member whose name is spoken

Understands and follows a simple direction

Notices sounds made by a clock, bell, whistle

Responds rhythmically to music with her whole body

Carries out instructions that include two steps

▲▽▲▽▲▽▲▽▲▽▲▽▲▽▲▽▲▽▲▽▲▽▲▽▲▽▲▽▲▽▲

Language and Cognitive Skills

▲▼▲▼▲▼▲▼▲▼▲▼▲▼▲▼▲▼▲▼▲▼▲▼▲▼▲▼▲▼▲▼▲▼▲▼▲▼

Jabbers with expression

Identifies pictures in a book

Uses single words meaningfully

Names objects when asked, "What's this?"

Uses twenty or more words

Names at least twenty-five familiar objects

Gestures to make his wants known

Names toys

Uses words to make wants known

Combines two different words

Tries to sing

Speaks in simple sentences

Finds familiar objects

Fits objects into containers

Turns two to three pages of a book at a time

Points to pictures in a book

Remembers where objects belong

Obtains a toy using a stick or a string

Self-Concept Skills

Demands personal attention

Points to parts of his body when identified

Insists on helping to feed herself

Names parts of a doll's body

Claims objects as his own

Refers to herself by name

Pulls on socks and mittens

Eats with a spoon

Drinks from a cup

Attempts to wash himself

Offers a toy but does not release it

Plays independently around another child

Enjoys short walks

Asks for food and water when needed

Block Games

▲▼▲▼▲▼▲▼▲▼▲▼▲▼▲▼▲▼▲▼▲▼▲▼▲▼▲▼▲▼▲▼▲▼▲

▲▼▲▼▲▼▲▼▲▼▲▼▲▼▲▼▲▼▲▼▲▼▲▼▲▼▲▼▲▼▲▼▲▼▲▼▲

Boom, Boom, Down

▲▼▲▼▲▼▲▼▲▼▲▼▲▼▲▼▲▼▲▼▲▼▲▼▲▼▲▼▲

▲ Toddlers adore piling up blocks and knocking them down.

▲ Help your child build a tower of blocks. Three or four is about all a toddler can stack because they can hardly refrain from knocking them over.

▲ When the blocks are stacked, say, "One and a two and a boom, boom, down!"

▲ On the word "down" knock down the blocks.

▲ After you have played this a few times, try stacking the blocks higher.

What your toddler will learn
▼
Fine motor skills

▲▼▲▼▲▼▲▼▲▼▲▼▲▼▲▼▲▼▲▼▲▼▲▼▲▼▲▼▲

block games ▲

More Block Games

▲▼▲▼▲▼▲▼▲▼▲▼▲▼▲▼▲▼▲▼▲▼▲▼▲▼▲▼▲

▲ Plastic bowls in different sizes are good beginning blocks because they are easy to manipulate and light in weight.

▲ Toddlers will enjoy trying to nest them in each other.

▲ You can also put the lids on the bowls and encourage toddlers to try stacking them.

▲ Through trial and error your child will soon learn that the bigger bowls go on the bottom.

▲ Trying to take the lids off the bowls and putting the lids back on the bowls will be a great challenge to your child.

▲ While you are playing with your child talk about concepts such as one bowl, two bowls, etc.

What your toddler will learn

▼

Fine motor skills

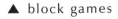

Disposable Blocks

▲▼▲▼▲▼▲▼▲▼▲▼▲▼▲▼▲▼▲▼▲▼▲▼▲▼▲

▲ Make disposable blocks out of small milk cartons.

▲ Tape all of the ends together and cover the cartons with contact paper.

▲ Let your toddler decorate the blocks with crayons or stickers.

▲ Play a stacking game with your toddler. Praise him each time he stacks one block on top of another.

▲ The most fun is to knock down the stacks.

▲ The great thing about these blocks is that you can throw them away when your child is no longer interested in playing with them.

What your toddler will learn
▼
Fine motor skills

▲▼▲▼▲▼▲▼▲▼▲▼▲▼▲▼▲▼▲▼▲▼▲▼▲▼▲

block games ▲

Milly, Molly, Mandy

▲▼▲▼▲▼▲▼▲▼▲▼▲▼▲▼▲▼▲▼▲▼▲▼▲▼▲▼▲

▲ This game requires a soft block.

▲ Sit on the floor with your toddler.

▲ Say the following.

> *Milly, Molly, Mandy*
>
> *Sweet as sugar candy*
>
> *Take the block and put it on the floor.*

▲ Show your toddler how to take the block and put it on the floor.

▲ Repeat the poem and tell your child to put the block on the table. Keep playing the game, changing the position of the block.

▲ When you think you child can do this easily, say the poem and give her two places to put the block.

> *Milly, Molly, Mandy*
>
> *Sweet as sugar candy*
>
> *Take the block and put it on the chair then put it on the sofa.*

What your toddler will learn

▼

To follow directions

▲ block games

One, One

▲ Sit on the floor with your toddler.

▲ Take three blocks and put them in front of you.

▲ Say, "One, one, this is fun." Take one block and move it in front of the other blocks. As you move it, say the words "one block." Move the block back to the others.

▲ Say, "Two, two, peekaboo." Take two blocks and move them in front of the other blocks. Say the words "two blocks" as you move them.

▲ Keep playing the game and moving the blocks.

>   *Three, three, shake your knee*

▲ When your child is ready, add, *"Four, four, knock at the door,"* and *"Five, five, sakes alive!"*

What your toddler will learn

▼

About numbers

The Bottom of the Sea

▲▼▲▼▲▼▲▼▲▼▲▼▲▼▲▼▲▼▲▼▲▼▲▼▲▼▲▼▲

▲ Sit on the floor with your toddler.

▲ Take three or four blocks and build a tower.

▲ Take a toy and put it on top of the blocks and tell your child, "The toy is on the top."

▲ Now ask your child to push the toy off of the top. Then tell your child, "The toy is on the bottom."

▲ Repeat the game letting your toddler do all of the work.

What your toddler will learn
▼
About top and bottom

▲▼▲▼▲▼▲▼▲▼▲▼▲▼▲▼▲▼▲▼▲▼▲▼▲▼▲▼▲

▲ block games

Four Little Blocks

▲ Take four different colored blocks and set them on the floor.

▲ As you put the blocks down say to your child, "One for mommy, one for daddy, one for doggie and one for you."

▲ Use family names that are meaningful to your child.

▲ As you say this rhyme, pick up each block and stack them.

Four pretty blocks are on the floor.

One, two, three, four. (point to the blocks as you count)

One for mommy, one for daddy, one for doggie too,

But the last block is just for you.

Jackie Silberg

▲ Now that you have stacked the blocks, repeat the poem and let your child take off the blocks one by one.

What your toddler will learn

▼

About counting and colors

block games ▲

Building a House

▲▼▲▼▲▼▲▼▲▼▲▼▲▼▲▼▲▼▲▼▲▼▲▼▲▼▲

▲ Sit on the floor with your toddler and lots of stackable blocks.

▲ Say the following poem, and put one block on top of another for each line of the poem.

> *Building a house, (put on first block)*
>
> *Start with the floor, (add next block)*
>
> *Two front windows, (add one more block)*
>
> *One front door. (add one more block)*
>
> *Put on the roof, (add one more block)*
>
> *Right at the top, (add one more block)*
>
> *Don't forget you've got to have a chimney pot. (add last block)*

▲ Say, "Let's knock the house down and start again."

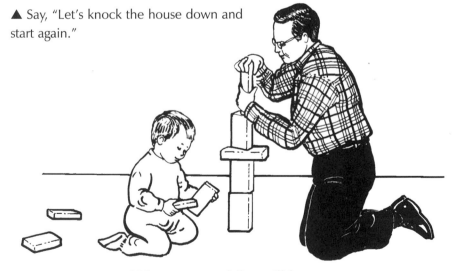

What your toddler will learn

▼

Fine motor skills

▲▼▲▼▲▼▲▼▲▼▲▼▲▼▲▼▲▼▲▼▲▼▲▼▲▼▲

▲ block games

The Farm Game

▲▼▲▼▲▼▲▼▲▼▲▼▲▼▲▼▲▼▲▼▲▼▲▼▲▼▲▼▲

▲ You will need plastic farm animals and blocks to play this game.

▲ Help your toddler make a circle with blocks.

▲ Say to your toddler, "Where is the cow?"

▲ Take the toy cow and put it in the block circle and say, "Moo moo."

▲ Take the toy cow out of the circle and give it to your toddler. Ask the question again, "Where is the cow?"

▲ Help your toddler put the toy cow in the circle and encourage him to say, "Moo, moo." The "m" sound is fairly common in beginning language, so this will be fairly easy for your child.

▲ Continue playing the game with different toy animals.

What your toddler will learn
▼
Language skills

▲▼▲▼▲▼▲▼▲▼▲▼▲▼▲▼▲▼▲▼▲▼▲▼▲▼▲▼▲

Bouncing Games

▲▼▲▼▲▼▲▼▲▼▲▼▲▼▲▼▲▼▲▼▲▼▲▼▲▼▲▼▲▼▲▼▲▼▲▼

Riding in the Buggy

▲▼▲▼▲▼▲▼▲▼▲▼▲▼▲▼▲▼▲▼▲▼▲▼▲▼▲

▲ Hold your child on your lap and bounce him.

▲ There are many ways to hold your child. You can have him face you, face outward with his back to you or bounce on your knee.

> *Riding in the buggy Mr. (child's name)*
>
> *(child's name), (child's name)*
>
> *Riding in the buggy Mr. (child's name)*
>
> *A long way from home.*

▲ Repeat the poem and change the word "buggy" to other transportation words. Car, train, horse and airplane are a few ideas.

What your toddler will learn

▼

Fun

▲▼▲▼▲▼▲▼▲▼▲▼▲▼▲▼▲▼▲▼▲▼▲▼▲▼▲

▲ bouncing games

Mrs. Sippy-0

▲▼▲▼▲▼▲▼▲▼▲▼▲▼▲▼▲▼▲▼▲▼▲▼▲▼▲

▲ Sit your toddler on your knees and say this bouncing rhyme.

▲ At the end of each verse, pick up your child and hold him high in the air.

> *Oh, Mrs. Sippy-o*
> *Had a little baby-o.*
> *She dressed it in calico*
> *Riding on a donkey.*
>
> *Oh, Mrs. Epplewhite*
> *Please come out tonight.*
> *You look a bonny sight*
> *Riding on a donkey.*

▲ Try making up your own verses and ending each one with "riding on a donkey."

What your toddler will learn

▼

Fun

▲▼▲▼▲▼▲▼▲▼▲▼▲▼▲▼▲▼▲▼▲▼▲▼▲▼▲

▲ bouncing games

Tom Sims

▲ This is an old English knee bouncing rhyme.

▲ Sit your toddler on your lap. Take her legs by the ankles and call one Bill Anderson and the other Tom Sims.

▲ Roll one leg over the other and move them faster and faster until the last line.

▲ On the last line, separate your knees and let your child slip down between them.

▲ Change the names of Bill Anderson and Tom Sims to names that your toddler will recognize.

> *This is Bill Anderson*
>
> *That is Tom Sims*
>
> *Tom called to Bill*
>
> *And fell over him*
>
> *Bill over Tom*
>
> *and Tom over Bill*
>
> *Over and over as they*
>
> *FELL DOWN THE HILL!*

▲ Let other members of the family take turns saying the same rhyme with your toddler.

What your toddler will learn

Fun

▲ bouncing games

Leg Over Leg

▲▼▲▼▲▼▲▼▲▼▲▼▲▼▲▼▲▼▲▼▲▼▲▼▲▼▲▼

▲ Cross your legs and bounce your toddler on your knee while holding her at the waist.

▲ When you get to the words "up, she went over," uncross your legs.

Leg over leg

The dog went to Dover.

When she got to the stile

Up, she went over.

▲ Repeat this rhyme several times. Each time you do it, raise your toddler higher in the air on the last line.

What your toddler will learn
▼
Listening skills

▲▼▲▼▲▼▲▼▲▼▲▼▲▼▲▼▲▼▲▼▲▼▲▼▲▼▲▼

▲ bouncing games

A Bouncing Game

▲ Sit your child on your lap facing you.

▲ Say the following rhyme as you bounce your knees up and down while holding your child at the waist.

▲ When you come to the words "fell in the gutter," separate your legs and drop your child to the ground while holding her tightly.

I went down town

To get some butter.

And when I got there

I fell in the gutter. (drop child down)

What your toddler will learn

▼

Rhythm

▲ bouncing games

This Is the Way

▲▼▲▼▲▼▲▼▲▼▲▼▲▼▲▼▲▼▲▼▲▼▲▼▲▼▲

▲ This is another version of a popular bouncing rhyme.

▲ Sit your toddler on your lap facing you.

▲ Hold him at the waist and bounce your legs up and down. Say the following rhyme.

> *This is the way the ladies ride*
>
> *Nimble nim, nimble nim*
>
> *This is the way the gentlemen ride*
>
> *Gallop-a-trot, gallop-a-trot*
>
> *This is the way the babies ride*
>
> *Jiggety jog, jiggety jog*
>
> *Till they fall in a ditch*
>
> *With a flippety flop*
>
> *Flop, flop, flop!*

▲ On the words "fall in a ditch," open up your knees and let your toddler drop down a bit while holding him securely.

What your toddler will learn

Trust

▲▼▲▼▲▼▲▼▲▼▲▼▲▼▲▼▲▼▲▼▲▼▲▼▲▼▲

▲ bouncing games

Kerplop!

▲▼▲▼▲▼▲▼▲▼▲▼▲▼▲▼▲▼▲▼▲▼▲▼▲▼▲

▲ This is a knee bouncing game.

▲ Sit your child on your knees and bounce up and down as you say the following rhyme.

▲ When you come to the word "kerplop," open up your knees and let your child fall through as you hold him.

> *Down by the banks of the Hanky Panks*
>
> *A bullfrog jumped from bank to bank.*
>
> *Where the eeps, ops, tiddly tops,*
>
> *Jumped around, and the bullfrog went*
>
> *Kerplop!*

What your toddler will learn

Trust

▲▼▲▼▲▼▲▼▲▼▲▼▲▼▲▼▲▼▲▼▲▼▲▼▲▼▲

37

▲ bouncing games

Trot, Trot to Boston Town

▲▼▲▼▲▼▲▼▲▼▲▼▲▼▲▼▲▼▲▼▲▼▲▼▲▼▲

▲ Here is a variation of a popular bouncing game.

▲ Sit your child on your lap facing you.

▲ Bounce him up and down.

▲ On the words "to the ground," open your legs and let your toddler drop down while you hold him tightly.

> *Trot, trot to Boston Town*
>
> *Drop that baby to the ground.*

▲ Start the rhyme very slowly and each time that you repeat it, increase the speed.

What your toddler will learn

▼

Anticipation

▲▼▲▼▲▼▲▼▲▼▲▼▲▼▲▼▲▼▲▼▲▼▲▼▲▼▲

▲ bouncing games

See Saw

▲ Sit your child in your lap facing you. It's easiest to play this game sitting on the floor.

▲ Hold your toddler at the waist and rock back and forth.

See saw, sacradown

Which is the way to London Town?

One foot up (raise your child's foot)

And one foot down (put her foot down)

That is the way to London Town.

See saw, Jack in the hedge

Which is the way to London Bridge?

Put on your shoes (shake your child's foot)

And away you trudge

This is the way to London Bridge.

▲ Open up your legs and while holding your child, let her drop between your legs as you say:

London Bridge?

Ohh, oh!

All fall down.

What your toddler will learn

Fun

▲ bouncing games

Bouncing Ball

▲▼▲▼▲▼▲▼▲▼▲▼▲▼▲▼▲▼▲▼▲▼▲▼▲▼

▲ Play this game with at least one other person.

▲ Say the following chant.

> *I'm a bouncing ball*
>
> *I'm a bouncing ball*
>
> *Bounce, bounce, bounce*
>
> *I'm a bouncing ball.*

▲ As you say the chant, pretend to bounce up and down. You can hold your toddler at the waist and bounce her until she gets the idea.

▲ Now tell your child that you are going to become a rolling ball.

▲ Sit down and arrange it so that there is a person at each end of the room.

▲ Tell your child, "I am going to roll you to daddy." Ready, set, go!"

▲ If necessary, gently give your child a start and let him roll over and over to the other end of the room.

▲ Your toddler will love it if you become the ball.

What your toddler will learn

▼

Coordination

▲▼▲▼▲▼▲▼▲▼▲▼▲▼▲▼▲▼▲▼▲▼▲▼▲▼

▲ bouncing games

Color & Shape

▲▽▲▽▲▽▲▽▲▽▲▽▲▽▲▽▲▽▲▽▲▽▲▽▲▽▲▽▲▽

Games

▲▽▲▽▲▽▲▽▲▽▲▽▲▽▲▽▲▽▲▽▲▽▲▽▲▽▲▽▲▽

Color Fun

▲ Take two small containers that are the same size. Margarine tubs work nicely.

▲ Paint or color one red and the other yellow. If you can find containers in these colors that would be even better.

▲ Put the containers in front of your child. Touch each container and say the color name.

▲ Take your child's hand and touch each container as you say the name again.

▲ Take the yellow container and say, "I like the yellow one."

▲ Ask your child, "Would you like the yellow one?" Give the container to your child.

▲ Continue taking a container and then giving it to your child.

▲ Put a small object in the yellow container. Hold up each container and shake it. Your child will get excited to see that one of the containers makes a noise.

▲ Ask your child to give you the yellow container.

▲ After you play this game a few times, your child will be able recognize the noisy container by the color.

What your toddler will learn
▼
About colors

color & shape games ▲

The Pushing Game

▲▼▲▼▲▼▲▼▲▼▲▼▲▼▲▼▲▼▲▼▲▼▲▼▲▼▲

▲ Take a coffee can with a lid and cut a slot in the top of the lid.

▲ Save several baby food jar lids for your toddler to push through the lid of the can.

▲ Children love to hear the "clank" as the lid hits the bottom of the can.

▲ Each time you give your child a lid to drop in the can, say, "Here is a circle to drop in the can."

▲ You could also cover the tops of the lids with red, yellow and blue construction paper. Each time you give your toddler a lid, say, "Here is a blue circle," or "Here is a red circle."

▲ If your child is not ready to put the lids through the slot, he will enjoy filling and dumping the can without the lid.

▲ This is an easy homemade toy that your child will love.

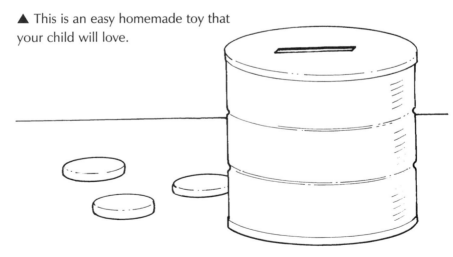

What your toddler will learn
▼
Fine motor skills

. ▼▲▼. ▼▲▼▲▼▲▼. .▼. .▼. .▼. ▼▲▼.   ▼▲▼. ▼▲▼▲▼▲▼▲

Artistry

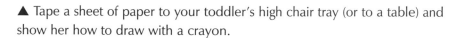

▲ Tape a sheet of paper to your toddler's high chair tray (or to a table) and show her how to draw with a crayon.

▲ Give her a large crayon. The kind that little hands can grasp easily.

▲ Let her experiment with marking the paper. Each time you give her a crayon, identify its color.

▲ Play a take-turn game. You make some wavy lines and then your toddler makes her lines.

▲ As she grows older, she will try to copy your marks. This is the time when she will begin to understand basic shapes.

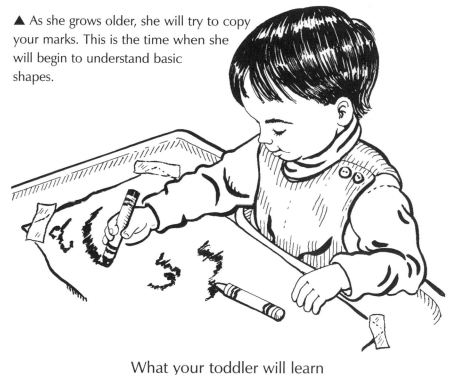

What your toddler will learn
▼
Fine motor skills

color & shape games ▲

Color Stickies

▲▼▲▼▲▼▲▼▲▼▲▼▲▼▲▼▲▼▲▼▲▼▲▼▲▼▲▼▲▼▲

▲ Get a roll of double-sided tape, the kind that is sticky on both sides.

▲ Make two balls out of the tape for you and your toddler. Give one of the balls to your child.

▲ Show her how it sticks to things by putting it on different parts of your body.

▲ Ask your child to take her ball and put it on her hand. Keep repeating the game with other parts of the body.

▲ Take two pieces of construction paper and put them in front of your child. The papers should be contrasting colors.

▲ Stick your ball on the red paper and say, "The ball is on the red paper. Can you stick your ball on the red paper?"

▲ Repeat with the second color.

What your toddler will learn
▼
About colors

▲▼▲▼▲▼▲▼▲▼▲▼▲▼▲▼▲▼▲▼▲▼▲▼▲▼▲▼▲▼▲

▲ color & shape games

Getting Dressed

▲ When it's time to get dressed, put your toddler's clothes in a pile on the floor.

▲ Ask your child to bring you the yellow shirt.

▲ If he brings it to you (chances are that he will), praise him and repeat what he brought to you. "What a good job! You brought the yellow shirt!"

▲ If he brings you another piece of clothing, say, "Thank you for bringing the blue pants." Put on the blue pants, and then ask him again to bring you the yellow shirt.

▲ Continue asking for each item one at a time. Name the item of clothing and the color.

▲ When your child can play this game easily, put the clothing in different places in the room. For example, "Bring me the red hat that's on the bed."

▲ This is a great self-esteem builder.

What your toddler will learn

▼

About colors

　　　　color & shape games ▲

Colors and Shapes

▲▼▲▼▲▼▲▼▲▼▲▼▲▼▲▼▲▼▲▼▲▼▲▼▲▼▲

▲ Cut out several circles from red construction paper.

▲ Put the circles on the floor in front of your toddler.

▲ Put your hands on the circles. Touch them one at a time.

▲ Say, "I am putting my hands on the red circle."

▲ Add yellow circles that you have previously cut out.

▲ Put your feet on the yellow circles and say, "I am putting my feet on the yellow circles."

▲ With your toddler, play this game of touching the red circles with your hands and the yellow circles with your feet.

What your toddler will learn
▼
About colors

▲▼▲▼▲▼▲▼▲▼▲▼▲▼▲▼▲▼▲▼▲▼▲▼▲▼▲

▲ color & shape games

The Fruit Salad Game

▲▼▲▼▲▼▲▼▲▼▲▼▲▼▲▼▲▼▲▼▲▼▲▼▲▼▲▼▲

▲ Gather together several fruits that are round. An apple, orange, peach, nectarine and grapes are perfect to play this game. Two fruits are enough to start this game.

▲ Say the following poem.

> *Round apples, round apples*
>
> *Yum, yum, yum*
>
> *I think I will get me some.*

▲ Ask your toddler to give you the round, red apple. If he is not sure, help him, then praise him for doing a good job.

▲ Put the apple in a bowl and say the rhyme again with the name of a different fruit.

> *Round grapes, round grapes*
>
> *Yum, yum, yum*
>
> *I think I will get me some.*

▲ Continue the game naming all of the round fruits.

▲ When you are finished, cut up the fruit and share a lovely fruit salad with your toddler.

What your toddler will learn

▼

About shapes

▲▼▲▼▲▼▲▼▲▼▲▼▲▼▲▼▲▼▲▼▲▼▲▼▲▼▲▼▲

color & shape games ▲

More Colors and Shapes

▲▼▲▼▲▼▲▼▲▼▲▼▲▼▲▼▲▼▲▼▲▼▲▼▲▼▲▼▲

▲ This game emphasizes shapes.

▲ Cut out squares and circles of the same color.

▲ Play the game of putting your hands on the circles.

▲ Put your feet on the squares.

▲ Play this game with your child.

> *Put your hands on the circle,*
>
> *Circle, circle.*
>
> *Hands on the circle,*
>
> *Just like me. (your child will copy you)*
>
> *Put your feet on the square,*
>
> *Square, square.*
>
> *Put your feet on the square,*
>
> *Just like me. (your child will copy you)*

What your toddler will learn

▼

About shapes

▲▼▲▼▲▼▲▼▲▼▲▼▲▼▲▼▲▼▲▼▲▼▲▼▲▼▲▼▲

▲ color & shape games

The Red Song

▲▼▲▼▲▼▲▼▲▼▲▼▲▼▲▼▲   ▲▼▲▼▲▼▲

▲ Sing about things that are red.

▲ Look around your house and find things that are red such as clothes, wallpaper, towels, whatever you can find.

▲ Show all the red things to your toddler. Name each one individually and say the color. "Look at the red shirt." "This is a red ball."

▲ Sing the Red Song to the tune of "London Bridge."

> (Child's name) has a red ball
>
> Red ball, red ball.
>
> (Child's name) has a red ball
>
> I love red!

▲ Sing about each thing that you have that is red.

▲ On another day, sing about a different color.

What your toddler will learn
▼
About colors

▲▼▲▼▲▼▲▼▲▼. .▼▲▼▲▼. .▼▲▼▲▼. .▼. .▼▲▼▲▼. .▼. .▼.

The Cookie Game

▲▼▲▼▲▼▲▼▲▼▲▼▲▼▲▼▲▼▲▼▲▼▲▼▲▼▲

▲ You will need red construction paper.

▲ Cut out two red circles. Decorate the circles to look like cookies.

▲ Sit on the floor with your toddler.

▲ Say the following poem.

> *One fine day in a cookie shop*
>
> *There were two little cookies with sugar on top.*
>
> *In came (child's name), hip hooray*
>
> *She picked up a red one and ran away.*

▲ Show your child the red one and tell her to run around the room when the words say "ran away."

▲ Continue the game using the word "red."

▲ As your toddler gets more experience with this game, add additional colors.

What your toddler will learn

▼

About colors

▲▼▲▼▲▼▲▼▲▼▲▼▲▼▲▼▲▼▲▼▲▼▲▼▲▼▲

▲ color & shape games

Mixing Colors

▲▼▲▼▲▼▲▼▲▼▲▼▲▼▲▼▲▼▲▼▲▼▲▼▲▼▲▼▲

▲ Talk about colors with your toddler. If you have a book about colors, read it to him.

▲ Take one of the three basic colors (red, yellow, blue) and walk around your house pointing out that color to your child.

▲ It's best to point out one color at a time.

▲ Play this game with another color on another day.

What your toddler will learn
▼
About colors

▲▼▲▼▲▼▲▼▲▼▲▼▲▼▲▼▲▼▲▼▲▼▲▼▲▼▲▼▲

color & shape games ▲

Blue Circle

▲▼▲▼▲▼▲▼▲▼▲▼▲▼▲▼▲▼▲▼▲▼▲▼▲▼▲▼▲▼▲▼▲

▲ Cut out circles, squares or triangles of two different colors. Start with blue, yellow or red.

▲ Lay the cut-out shapes on a table in front of you and your toddler.

▲ Start with the blue circle.

▲ Pick it up and place it in front of you.

▲ As you move the circle, say, "Blue circle."

▲ Pick up a second blue circle and say, "Blue circle."

▲ Point to each circle and say, "One, two, I love you."

▲ After you have done a few, ask your child if she knows where a blue circle is.

▲ Another day do this game with triangles or squares.

What your toddler will learn

▼

About shapes

▲▼▲▼▲▼▲▼▲▼▲▼▲▼▲▼▲▼▲▼▲▼▲▼▲▼▲▼▲▼▲▼▲

Spots and Stripes

▲ Find pieces of material or articles of clothing that have spots and stripes on them.

▲ Show your toddler the spots. Touch them, count them or trace your finger around them. Let him become familiar with the shape and the name.

▲ Do the same with the striped material.

▲ Draw spots and stripes on paper and let your child tell you which are the spots and which are the stripes.

▲ Walk around the house and look for spots and stripes. Many times you will find them on walls or floors as well as canned goods.

▲ Look at an animal picture book. Find animals with spots or stripes.

What your toddler will learn
▼
Observation skills

color & shape games ▲

Language Games

Sounds Are Fun

▲ Look at your toddler and make vowel sounds. Say each vowel several times and then stop and see if your child will copy you.

▲ Say the vowel sounds in different pitches. Say them high and say them low. Say them fast and say them slowly.

▲ Combine two vowel sounds, for example "ee, ee, ee, ah, ah, ah."

▲ Make up melodies to go with the vowel sounds.

▲ The more that you play with sounds, the more your child will enjoy the sounds that he makes too.

▲ This is a beginning step in developing a positive attitude about words and eventually reading.

What your toddler will learn
▼
About sounds

language games ▲

The Pretend House

▲▼▲▼▲▼▲▼▲▼▲▼▲▼▲▼▲▼▲▼▲▼▲▼▲▼▲▼▲

▲ Use boxes, pillows and sheets to make a tunnel.

▲ Show your toddler how to crawl through the tunnel.

▲ Tell her, "Let's crawl into the house."

▲ Start crawling and encourage her to follow you.

▲ As you are crawling say, "We are inside the house."

▲ When you get to the other end, say, "Now we are outside the house."

▲ Go back into the tunnel house and say, "Now we are inside the house."

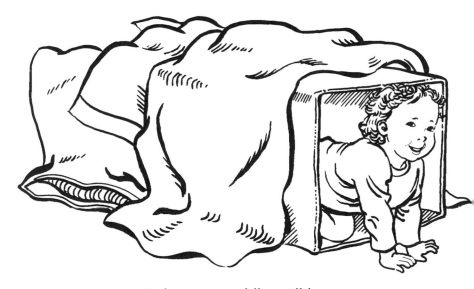

What your toddler will learn
▼
Coordination

▲▼▲▼▲▼▲▼▲▼▲▼▲▼▲▼▲▼▲▼▲▼▲▼▲▼▲▼▲

▲ language games

Changing Sounds

▲ This is a good game to develop your toddler's listening skills.

▲ Sit your child in your lap facing you.

▲ Start saying the same sound over and over. For example, "da, da, da, etc."

▲ Now change the sound to something else like "ga, ga, ga, etc."

▲ If you notice a reaction when you change sounds, it shows that she is listening carefully.

▲ Go back to the first sound and as you say it, change the pitch of your voice.

▲ When she seems to get bored with this, change to the second sound and change your voice pitch at the same time.

▲ If she responds with a smile or excitement you know that she is listening intently.

▲ End the game with a big hug.

What your toddler will learn
▼
Listening skills

My Name

▲▼▲▼▲▼▲▼▲▼▲▼▲▼▲▼▲▼▲▼▲▼▲▼▲▼▲▼▲▼▲

▲ When toddlers are learning to talk, they sometimes call other people by their own name because they haven't yet associated their own name with themselves. This is a game that will help them realize their name belongs to them.

▲ Say the name of an object in the room, for example, "table."

▲ Take your toddler's hand and as you say the word "table" put her hand on the table. Then say, "(Toddler's name) is touching the table."

▲ Touch the table and say, "Daddy is touching the table."

▲ Repeat this game with a total of three words, for example, table, chair and block.

▲ Now go back to the beginning and repeat and touch each object again.

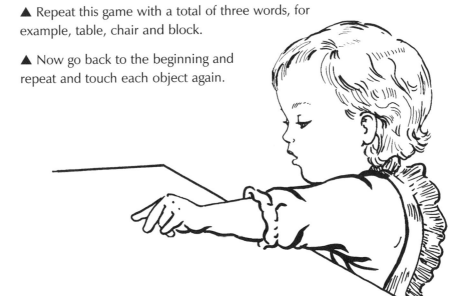

What your toddler will learn
▼
Name recognition

▲▼▲▼▲▼▲▼▲▼▲▼▲▼▲▼▲▼▲▼▲▼▲▼▲▼▲▼▲▼▲

▲ language games

Blowing

▲ Sit your toddler in your lap and touch her lips. As you touch her lips say the word "lips."

▲ Take your child's fingers and put them on your lips and say the words, "(mommy's) lips."

▲ Take your lips and blow a stream of air on your toddler's palm.

▲ Put some torn up tissue paper on a table and show your toddler how you can blow it around.

▲ Encourage your child to copy you and to blow.

▲ Play a game of counting. One, two, three, blow.

What your toddler will learn
▼
Observation skills

language games ▲

A Remarkable Discovery

▲▼▲▼▲▼▲▼▲▼▲▼▲▼▲▼▲▼▲▼▲▼▲▼▲▼▲▼

▲ Toddlers enjoy learning how to identify the different parts of their bodies. The most remarkable part of this discovery is that they learn that they are a person just like you.

▲ Stand in front of a mirror with your child.

▲ Point to his nose and say, "Here is (child's name's) nose. Now point to your nose and say, "Here is daddy's nose."

▲ Turn your child around facing you and ask him to touch your nose.

▲ When he touches your nose say, "Your nose is just like daddy's nose."

▲ Continue the game with a different part of the body.

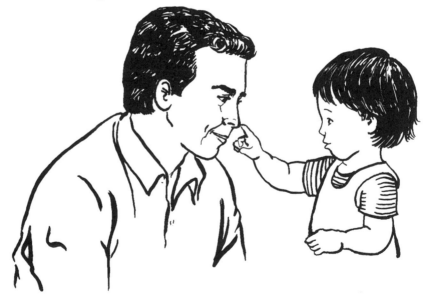

What your toddler will learn
▼
About parts of the body

▲▼▲▼▲▼▲▼▲▼▲▼▲▼▲▼▲▼▲▼▲▼▲▼▲▼▲▼

▲ language games

Where Is It?

▲ Sit on the floor next to your toddler.

▲ Put a box in front of the two of you.

▲ Take a stuffed animal and put it next to the box. As you do this, tell your child that you are putting the toy next to the box.

▲ Now, ask your toddler to give you the toy that is next to the box.

▲ Continue by putting the stuffed animal in front of the box, behind the box, on top of the box and under the box.

▲ Next, give the toy to your child and ask her to put the toy in different places around the box.

▲ When your child does this easily, add more boxes so that the game will become more challenging.

What your toddler will learn
▼
About spatial concepts

▲▼▲▼▲▼▲▼▲▼▲▼▲▼▲▼▲▼▲▼▲▼▲▼▲▼▲

language games ▲

Fill in the Word

▲▼▲▼▲▼▲▼▲▼▲▼▲▼▲▼▲▼▲▼▲▼▲▼▲▼▲▼

▲ Toddlers at this age can usually say a few words like "mama," "dada" and their own name.

▲ Make up a story with your child's name in the story. Each time you come to her name, let her fill in the word.

▲ For example, "Once upon a time there was a little girl named (your child's name). This little girl named _____ (let child fill in the word) went to the kitchen to eat her lunch." Keep making up the story and each time say, "This little girl named _____."

▲ Your child will really love playing this game as young children love to hear their names in stories.

Once upon a Time...

What your toddler will learn

▼

Name recognition

▲▼▲▼▲▼▲▼▲▼▲▼▲▼▲▼▲▼▲▼▲▼▲▼▲▼▲▼

▲ language games

The Push-Pull Game

▲▼▲▼▲▼▲▼▲▼▲▼▲▼▲▼▲▼▲▼▲▼▲▼▲▼▲

▲ Show your toddler how to push a toy car along the floor.

▲ "Toot, Toot, here comes the car." Play pushing cars with your child.

▲ Tie a string to the car and show her how to pull the car.

▲ Take a box and cut a hole in it for the tunnel. Place it on the floor.

▲ Say to your toddler, "Here comes the car through the tunnel."

▲ Push the car through the hole.

▲ Give your child directions to push the car or pull the car.

▲ Show your toddler how to push things using a cardboard tube from a paper towel roll. Try pushing a ball.

What your toddler will learn
▼
About pushing and pulling

▲▼▲▼▲▼▲▼▲▼▲▼▲▼▲▼▲▼▲▼▲▼▲▼▲▼▲

Up and Down

▲▼▲▼▲▼▲▼▲▼▲▼▲▼▲▼▲▼▲▼▲▼▲▼▲▼▲▼▲▼▲

▲ Understanding the correct placement of objects can be practiced by turning your toddler's favorite objects upside down.

▲ Take a stuffed animal and stand it on its head.

▲ See if your child understands how to set it right side up.

▲ Sing the following song to your child to the tune of "Are You Sleeping?"

> *Turn it over, turn it over. (turn over the stuffed animal)*
>
> *Stand it up, stand it up. (put it back correctly)*
>
> *(child's name) turned it over, (help child turn over the toy)*
>
> *(child's name) turned it over.*
>
> *Stand it up, stand it up. (help child put it back)*

▲ Play the game with different objects in the house. Pots, cups, sealed boxes of cereal and books are good to start with.

What your toddler will learn
▼
About spatial concepts

▲▼▲▼▲▼▲▼▲▼▲▼▲▼▲▼▲▼▲▼▲▼▲▼▲▼▲▼▲▼▲

The Three Bears

▲▼▲▼▲▼▲▼▲▼▲▼▲▼▲▼▲▼▲▼▲▼▲▼▲▼▲

▲ Show your toddler pictures of bears or go to the zoo to see a bear.

▲ Tell your child a very shortened story of "The Three Bears."

▲ Change your voice for the Papa bear, Mama bear and Baby bear.

▲ After you have told the story once, tell it again and encourage your toddler to participate in the story.

▲ The best way to encourage your toddler to participate in the story is to leave out one word for her to fill in.

Somebody has been sleeping in my ____.

▲ You will see how quickly she will start saying the word "bed."

What your toddler will learn

▼

Language skills

▲▼▲▼▲▼▲▼▲▼▲▼▲▼▲▼▲▼▲▼▲▼▲▼▲▼▲

language games ▲

What Animal?

▲ You will need small plastic animals for this game.

▲ Look at each animal with your toddler. Talk about the name of the animal and the sound that it makes.

▲ Put all of the animals in a large container.

▲ Tell your toddler to put his hand in the container and take out an animal.

▲ When he has taken the animal out of the container, ask him to identify it by name and tell you the sound that it makes.

▲ Take turns playing this.

▲ When you feel that your child knows all of the animals, try tricking him. Name the animal, but purposely make the wrong sound. For example, take out a horse and say, "Quack, quack."

What your toddler will learn
▼
Language skills

Listen to the Sound

▲▼▲▼▲▼▲▼▲▼▲▼▲▼▲▼▲▼▲▼▲▼▲▼▲▼▲▼▲

▲ There are many sounds inside and outside. It is important to help a toddler begin to differentiate the sounds.

▲ Take a sound walk through your house and point out the different sounds to your child.

▲ You will be amazed yourself at all the sounds in your home.

▲ Here are some sounds that you might hear.

Radio playing	*Dishwasher running*
Rain falling	*Refrigerator running*
Doorbell ringing	*Sirens blaring*
Computer humming	*Toilet flushing*
Lights buzzing	*Clock ticking*
Dog barking	*Furnace running*
Telephone ringing	*Birds singing*
Person coughing	

What your toddler will learn
▼
Listening skills

▲▼▲▼▲▼▲▼▲▼▲▼▲▼▲▼▲▼▲▼▲▼▲▼▲▼▲▼▲

language games ▲

Making Faces

▲▽▲▽▲▽▲▽▲▽▲▽▲▽▲▽▲▽▲▽▲▽▲▽▲▽▲▽▲▽▲

▲ Imitating the sounds and words that your toddler makes is a very good way to communicate with her.

▲ When she starts to talk, copy her words and say the same thing.

▲ When you have her attention, make a funny face like crinkling your nose.

▲ Encourage her to make the same face.

▲ Here are some ideas for faces that you can make. Accompany each face with a sound. Twist your lips in different ways.

Sad face

Happy face

Surprised face

Scary face

What your toddler will learn

▼

Observation skills

▲▽▲▽▲▽▲▽▲▽▲▽▲▽▲▽▲▽▲▽▲▽▲▽▲▽▲▽▲▽▲

▲ language games

Find the Chair

▲▼▲▼▲▼▲▼▲▼▲▼▲▼▲▼▲▼▲▼▲▼▲▼▲▼▲

▲ Cut out pictures from magazines of objects in your house such as tables, chairs, beds, refrigerator, sink, toilet, etc.

▲ Show the pictures to your toddler and talk about them.

▲ Put all of the pictures in a box. Let your child pick one of them out.

▲ Ask her what is in the picture. If it is a bed, say to her, "Where is your bed?" Take her to the room that has the bed and let her show you the bed.

▲ Continue naming each picture and finding a matching item in your house.

▲ Once your child can identify the pictures, you make it a little harder by showing pictures of things that are in closets or drawers.

What your child will learn
▼
Thinking skills

▲▼▲▼▲▼▲▼▲▼▲▼▲▼▲▼▲▼▲▼▲▼▲▼▲

Sharing Books

▲ Although this is in the 21-24 month section, reading books to your child is important from birth.

▲ Remember that toddlers don't sit still very long. Your child may look at a book with you, walk away for awhile and then come back.

▲ Toddlers are interested in books about moms and dads, families, going to bed, how things work, animals and babies, sitting on a potty, bugs and more.

▲ Look for illustrations that are filled with wonderful information. Talking about the pictures encourages language skills.

▲ Toddlers like books that are repetitive, that rhyme and that are predictable.

▲ See the appendix for a recommended list of books for toddlers.

What your toddler will learn
▼
A love of reading

Whispering

▲▼▲▼▲▼▲▼▲▼▲▼▲▼▲▼▲▼▲▼▲▼▲▼▲▼▲

▲ Toddlers are fascinated by whispering. They are very proud of themselves when they can do it.

▲ Whispering helps children learn to modulate their voice. It takes a lot of concentration.

▲ Whisper something to your toddler. Say, "Let's read a book."

▲ Ask your toddler to whisper something back to you.

▲ Keep whispering to each other until your toddler understands how to make her voice very soft.

What your toddler will learn
▼
About sounds

language games ▲

Friends for Breakfast

▲▼▲▼▲▼▲▼▲▼▲▼▲▼▲▼▲▼▲▼▲▼▲▼▲▼▲▼▲

▲ Pretending with toddlers is fun for both you and your child. It also paves the way for imagination development and creative thinking.

▲ Invite your child's stuffed animals to breakfast. Sit them around your child and pretend to feed the animals.

▲ Ask the guests questions such as, "Do you like orange juice?" or "How does the cereal taste?" Answer the questions in different voices.

▲ Soon you will see your child pretending with his stuffed friends.

What your toddler will learn

▼

Creativity

▲▼▲▼▲▼▲▼▲▼▲▼▲▼▲▼▲▼▲▼▲▼▲▼▲▼▲▼▲

Who Ever Saw?

▲▼▲▼▲▼▲▼▲▼▲▼▲▼▲▼▲▼▲▼▲▼▲▼▲▼▲

▲ Say the following in two voices. One for you and one for the cat. Change your voice so the different voices will be very apparent to your toddler.

> Person: *Where are you going my little cat?*
>
> Cat: *I'm going to town to get me a hat!*
>
> Person: *What, a hat for a cat! A cat with a hat! Who ever saw a cat with a hat?*
>
> Cat: *Meow, meow, meow.*

▲ Here is another version.

> Person: *Where are you going my little kittens?*
>
> Kittens: *We're going to town to get us some mittens.*
>
> Person: *What, mittens for kittens! Do kittens wear mittens? Who ever saw little kittens with mittens?*
>
> Kittens: *Meow, meow, meow.*

What your toddler will learn
▼
Imagination

▲▼▲▼▲▼▲▼▲▼▲▼▲▼▲▼▲▼▲▼▲▼▲▼▲▼▲

A Box Story

▲ You will need a square box large enough to glue pictures on all of the sides. Gift boxes work well.

▲ Cut pictures from magazines that have familiar objects on them.

▲ Paste the pictures on the sides of the box.

▲ Lay down on the floor with your toddler. Touch one side of the box and start telling a story about the pictures on the box.

▲ Turn the box around and start telling another story.

▲ This will encourage your child to do the same thing when he is playing. This game really helps your child develop language skills.

▲ You could also paste pictures from your child's favorite story on the box.

▲ If you make several of these, they could be stacked as blocks.

What your child will learn
▼
Language skills

Tongue Twister

▲▼▲▼▲▼▲▼▲▼▲▼▲▼▲▼▲▼▲▼▲▼▲▼▲▼▲▼▲

▲ One of the first sounds that your toddler makes is the "b" sound. The following tongue twister is fun for your child to hear and he will probably try to imitate you.

> *Betty Botter bought some butter*
>
> *But, she said, "the butter's bitter.*
>
> *If I put it in my batter*
>
> *It will make my batter bitter*
>
> *But a bit of better butter*
>
> *That would make my batter better."*

▲ Repeat this in a sing-song rhythmic sound so that your child can hear the rhythm of the poem.

▲ Say the twister in different voices. A high voice, a low voice, a soft voice and a whiny voice.

▲ The more variations that you present to your child, the more he will want to play with language.

What your toddler will learn
▼
Language skills

▲▼▲▼▲▼▲▼▲▼▲▼▲▼▲▼▲▼▲▼▲▼▲▼▲▼▲▼▲

language games ▲

The Catalog Game

▲▽▲▽▲▽▲▽▲▽▲▽▲▽▲▽▲▽▲▽▲▽▲▽▲▽▲▽▲▽▲

▲ Select a catalog with a variety of pictures of things with which your child is familiar.

▲ Take turns picking something for the other person to be, for example, a dog.

▲ If you pick a picture of a dog, then your toddler has to pretend to be a dog.

▲ Another idea is to tape pictures on 3 x 5 cards and turn this into a card game.

What your toddler will learn

▼

Language skills

▲▽▲▽▲▽▲▽▲▽▲▽▲▽▲▽▲▽▲▽▲▽▲▽▲▽▲▽▲▽▲

 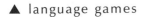

Guess the Sound

▲▼▲▼▲▼▲▼▲▼▲▼▲▼▲▼▲▼▲▼▲▼▲▼▲▼▲▼▲

▲ Talk with your toddler about different sounds. Ask questions about different animal sounds.

▲ What does the cow say? What does the car say? Go over sounds with which your child is familiar.

▲ Say the following rhyme.

> *Guess what is making the sound I hear:*
>
> *Moo, moo, moo (make the sound of a cow)*
>
> *A cow is making the sound I hear.*

▲ Repeat the poem again saying the same words.

▲ Repeat the poem and see if your toddler can fill in the word "cow."

▲ This rhyme can be changed for any sound.

What your toddler will learn

▼

Language skills

▲▼▲▼▲▼▲▼▲▼▲▼▲▼▲▼▲▼▲▼▲▼▲▼▲▼▲▼▲

language games ▲

Family Outing

▲▼▲▼▲▼▲▼▲▼▲▼▲▼▲▼▲▼▲▼▲▼▲▼▲▼▲▼▲

▲ Taking your toddler to a variety of places develops speaking, thinking and reading skills.

▲ A local farmer's market is a wonderful place to visit.

▲ Look at all of the fruits and vegetables. Touch them, smell them, talk about their color.

▲ Pick some fruits and vegetables, then go home and prepare them for eating.

What your toddler will learn

▼

Language skills

▲▼▲▼▲▼▲▼▲▼▲▼▲▼▲▼▲▼▲▼▲▼▲▼▲▼▲▼

▲ language games

Outside Games

▲▽▲▽▲▽▲▽▲▽▲▽▲▽▲▽▲▽▲▽▲▽▲▽▲▽▲▽▲▽▲▽▲▽▲

▲▽▲▽▲▽▲▽▲▽▲▽▲▽▲▽▲▽▲▽▲▽▲▽▲▽▲▽▲▽▲▽▲▽▲

Here's a Ball

▲▼▲▼▲▼▲▼▲▼▲▼▲▼▲▼▲▼▲▼▲▼▲▼▲▼▲▼▲

▲ Play this game outside.

▲ Take three balls and put them next to one another. The balls should be small, medium and large.

▲ Show each ball to your toddler and roll it on the ground. Ask your toddler to retrieve it.

▲ Show your toddler the small ball. Put your thumb and index finger together to make a circle. Say to your toddler, "Just like the small ball."

▲ Show your toddler the medium ball. Put your two thumbs together and your two index fingers together and say, "Just like the bigger ball."

▲ Show your toddler the large ball. Put your hands together over your head to make a big ball. Say, "Just like the biggest ball."

▲ Roll each ball to your toddler again. Ask her to retrieve each one.

What your toddler will learn

▼

About sizes

▲▼▲▼▲▼▲▼▲▼▲▼▲▼▲▼▲▼▲▼▲▼▲▼▲▼▲▼▲

outside games ▲

Alley, Alley, Alley, Oh!

▲▼▲▼▲▼▲▼▲▼▲▼▲▼▲▼▲▼▲▼▲▼▲▼▲▼▲▼▲

▲ Hold your child in your arms and say the following rhyme.

> *Alley, alley, alley, oh, (sway back and forth)*
>
> *'Round and around and around we go. (spin around while holding your toddler)*
>
> *Alley, alley, alley, oh, (sway back and forth)*
>
> *'Round and around and around we go. (spin around again)*
>
> *Alley, alley, alley, I, (sway back and forth)*
>
> *Fly like a bird in the sky. (hold your toddler in a horizontal position and fly around)*
>
> *Alley, alley, alley, I, (repeat action)*
>
> *Fly like a bird in the sky. (repeat action)*
>
> *Alley, alley, alley, E, (sway back and forth)*
>
> *Swim like a fish in the deep blue sea. (hold your toddler horizontally low to the ground and pretend to be a fish)*
>
> *Alley, alley, alley, E, (repeat action)*
>
> *Swim like a fish in the deep blue sea. (repeat action)*
>
> Jackie Silberg

What your toddler will learn
▼
Language skills

▲ outside games

Ducky Daddles

▲▼▲▼▲▼▲▼▲▼▲▼▲▼▲▼▲▼▲▼▲▼▲▼▲▼▲▼▲▼▲

▲ Show your toddler how to walk like a duck. Walk around saying, "Quack, quack."

▲ Say the following poem.

> *Ducky Daddles*
>
> *Loves the puddles*
>
> *How he waddles*
>
> *As he paddles*
>
> *In the puddles*
>
> *Ducky Daddles*

▲ Say the poem one line at a time. Let your toddler waddle around.

▲ Ask him to stop waddling when you stop speaking. After every line say, "Quack, quack," then stop speaking. See how long it takes for your toddler to stop waddling.

What your toddler will learn
▼
Listening skills

▲▼▲▼▲▼▲▼▲▼▲▼▲▼▲▼▲▼▲▼▲▼▲▼▲▼▲▼▲▼▲

outside games ▲

Pushing Fun

▲▼▲▼▲▼▲▼▲▼▲▼▲▼▲▼▲▼▲▼▲▼▲▼▲▼▲▼▲

▲ Toddlers love to push things. This game develops their upper arm strength.

▲ Strollers are a favorite thing to push.

▲ Many supermarkets have child size shopping carts for toddlers.

▲ The following poem is a good pushing game to play outside with a stroller, a child's shopping cart or a wagon.

> Push, push, push, push. (child pushes stroller, car, etc.)
>
> One, two, STOP. (stop pushing)
>
> Look around and what do you see? (encourage your child to look around)
>
> I see a tree smiling at me. (point to the tree)
>
> Now it's time to push again,
>
> Ready, set, GO.

▲ Repeat over and over. Instead of "a tree smiling at me," change the word each time.

What your toddler will learn
▼
Observation skills

▲▼▲▼▲▼▲▼▲▼▲▼▲▼▲▼▲▼▲▼▲▼▲▼▲▼▲▼▲

Megaphone

▲▼▲▼▲▼▲▼▲▼▲▼▲▼▲▼▲▼▲▼▲▼▲▼▲▼▲

▲ This is a great outside game because you can yell.

▲ Make a megaphone by rolling a large sheet of paper into a cone and taping the ends.

▲ Sit down with your toddler and speak loudly in the megaphone. "Hello everybody, how are you?"

▲ Now give the megaphone to your child and let her speak loudly into the megaphone.

▲ Hold the megaphone again and repeat the same words but this time speak very softly.

▲ Give the megaphone to your child and encourage her to speak softly.

▲ Say words into the megaphone that your toddler can say. Some of them might be: mama, dada, car, light, bye-bye and ball.

▲ Keep saying a word and then giving the megaphone to your child to say a word.

What your toddler will learn
▼
About loud and soft

▲▼▲▼▲▼▲▼▲▼▲▼▲▼▲▼▲▼▲▼▲▼▲▼▲▼▲

outside games ▲

Butterfly

▲▼▲▼▲▼▲▼▲▼▲▼▲▼▲▼▲▼▲▼▲▼▲▼▲▼▲▼▲▼▲

▲ Show your toddler pictures of butterflies.

▲ Go outside and look for butterflies. Talk about how beautiful they look as they flutter from one place to another.

▲ Say the following rhyme with your child as you dance around and pretend to be a butterfly.

> *Butterfly, butterfly*
>
> *Why do you flutter by?*
>
> *Butterfly, butterfly*
>
> *Where do you fly?*

▲ Tell your child that you are going to be butterflies and flutter to a tree. As you flutter to the tree say, "Flutter, flutter, flutter."

▲ Flutter to other outside places.

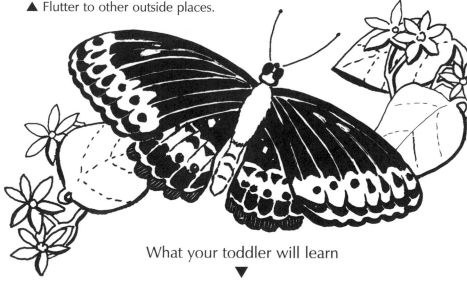

What your toddler will learn

▼

About nature

▲▼▲▼▲▼▲▼▲▼▲▼▲▼▲▼▲▼▲▼▲▼▲▼▲▼▲▼▲▼▲

Baby Bird

▲▼▲▼▲▼▲▼▲▼▲▼▲▼▲▼▲▼▲▼▲▼▲▼▲▼▲▼▲

▲ This is a nice game to play outside in warm weather.

▲ Sit down on the grass and have your toddler curl up in your lap.

▲ You pretend to be the big bird and your toddler is the baby bird.

▲ Pretend to be asleep and then wake up. Say to your child, "Come on, baby bird it's time to fly." Very slowly get up and flap your arms like wings. Fly around the yard and then say to your toddler, "Let's fly to the tree." Give specific directions to help your toddler learn the names of objects in the yard.

▲ Whisper to your baby bird, "It's time to go back to the nest."

▲ Go back to where you were sitting, and let your baby bird curl back into your arms.

▲ Repeat this game over and over. You might even ask your baby bird to fly by himself, then come back to the nest.

What your toddler will learn
▼
Bonding

outside games ▲

Things to Do

▲▼▲▼▲▼▲▼▲▼▲▼▲▼▲▼▲▼▲▼▲▼▲▼▲▼▲▼▲

▲ Say the following poem and do the actions with your child.

> Up and down, (move hands up and down)
>
> Round and round, (roll your hands in a circle)
>
> Pick a flower from the ground. (pretend to pick a flower)
>
> Run with the wind, (run in place)
>
> Swim in the sea, (pretend to swim)
>
> Climb up a rope, (pretend to climb)
>
> And buzz like a bee. (buzz and fly around)
>
> Buzz, buzz, buzz, buzz, buzz.
>
> Jackie Silberg

What your toddler will learn

▼

Coordination

▲▼▲▼▲▼▲▼▲▼▲▼▲▼▲▼▲▼▲▼▲▼▲▼▲▼▲▼▲

Cuckoo Clock

▲▼▲▼▲▼▲▼▲▼▲▼▲▼▲▼▲▼▲▼▲▼▲▼▲▼▲▼

▲ This game can be played indoors or outdoors. If you are playing outside, find a low branch of a tree that you can reach.

▲ Hold your child in your arms and sway back and forth.

> *Tick, tock, tick, tock,*
>
> *I'm a little cuckoo clock.*
>
> *Now I'm striking one o'clock,*
>
> *Cuckoo.*

▲ On the word "cuckoo" bring your child up over your head.

▲ If you are outside and there is a low branch that you can reach, sit your child on the branch (holding your child, of course) and tell him to sing like a cuckoo bird.

What your toddler will learn

▼

Language skills

▲▼▲▼▲▼▲▼▲▼▲▼▲▼▲▼▲▼▲▼▲▼▲▼▲▼▲▼

outside games ▲

Texture Feet

▲▼▲▼▲▼▲▼▲▼▲▼▲▼▲▼▲▼▲▼▲▼▲▼▲▼▲▼▲

▲ Chances are your toddler loves to take off her shoes and walk barefoot.

▲ With guided supervision, this is a wonderful sensory experience for your child.

▲ Walk with her on different surfaces and talk about each one.

▲ Grass, sand, crunchy leaves, warm sidewalk, mud, stones and water are all fascinating to feel on a bare foot.

▲ Talk about how the surfaces feel. Use words like cool, hard, soft, smooth, wet.

What your toddler will learn
▼
About textures

▲▼▲▼▲▼▲▼▲▼▲▼▲▼▲▼▲▼▲▼▲▼▲▼▲▼▲▼▲

▲ outside games

Five Little Birds

▲▼▲▼▲▼▲▼▲▼▲▼▲▼▲▼▲▼▲▼▲▼▲▼▲▼▲

▲ This is a nice fingerplay about birds.

▲ Go outside and talk about the birds. Watch them fly, listen to them chirp and enjoy their beauty.

▲ Tell your child that birds live in the trees.

▲ Look for a bird nest.

> *Five little birds without any home. (hold up five fingers of one hand)*
>
> *Five little trees in a row. (raise your hand high over your head)*
>
> *Come build your nest in our branches tall. (cup your other hand for the nest and place the fingers in it)*
>
> *We'll rock you to and fro. (rock both hands together)*

What your toddler will learn

▼

Fine motor skills

▲▼▲▼▲▼▲▼▲▼▲▼▲▼▲▼▲▼▲▼▲▼▲▼▲▼▲

outside games ▲

Colored Water Fun

▲▼▲▼▲▼▲▼▲▼▲▼▲▼▲▼▲▼▲▼▲▼▲▼▲▼▲

▲ This is a good outside or bathtub game.

▲ Take several see-through plastic jars and fill them with colored water.

▲ The jars should be small enough that little hands can hold them.

▲ Show your toddler how to pour the contents of one jar into the other.

▲ Not only will your toddler gain practice in motor skills, but he will see the color of the water change hues.

What your toddler will learn
▼
Fine motor skills

▲▼▲▼▲▼▲▼▲▼▲▼▲▼▲▼▲▼▲▼▲▼▲▼▲▼▲

Car Talk

▲ This is a good game to occupy your toddler in the car and develop her language at the same time.

▲ Take a pretend phone in the car with you.

▲ Ask your child to call the supermarket and ask them if they have any carrots.

▲ Ask your child to call the library and ask if they have her favorite book.

▲ Ask your child to call the gas station and ask if they have any gas.

▲ Give your child different places to call and ask questions about things with which she is familiar.

What your toddler will learn
▼
Language skills

outside games ▲

Shadow Play

▲▼▲▼▲▼▲▼▲▼▲▼▲▼▲▼▲▼▲▼▲▼▲▼▲▼▲▼▲

▲ Take your toddler outside on a sunny day and show her shadows.

▲ Walk around the yard or a park and observe the shadows of the trees, building, etc.

▲ Show her your shadow. Tell her to stand on your shadow.

▲ Ask her to jump over your shadow. Step on her shadow.

▲ Draw a chalk line around a shadow cast on a sidewalk.

▲ Draw a line in the dirt with a stick around a shadow cast in dirt.

What your toddler will learn
▼
Observation skills

▲▼▲▼▲▼▲▼▲▼▲▼▲▼▲▼▲▼▲▼▲▼▲▼▲▼▲▼▲

▲ outside games

Balancing

▲ Balance beams are fun to walk on and challenging to a toddler.

▲ Many parks or playgrounds have beams low enough for your child to walk on, or try walking across a curb or a log secured in the ground.

▲ Walk across the balance beam as your child watches.

▲ Take his hands and hold him as he walks across the beam.

▲ Soon your child will want to try it by himself.

▲ Take a favorite toy and put it at one end of the beam. Encourage your toddler to walk across and retrieve the toy.

What your toddler will learn
▼
Balance

outside games ▲

One, Two, Three!

▲▼▲▼▲▼▲▼▲▼▲▼▲▼▲▼▲▼▲▼▲▼▲▼▲▼▲▼▲

▲ This is a good car game. Every time the car stops, clap three times.

▲ As you clap, count, "One, two, three."

▲ Let your toddler say the word "three." You say, "One, two" and she says, "Three."

▲ This game takes a lot of concentration. Your child is clapping (coordination), speaking (language skills) and paying attention to when the car stops (cognitive skills).

▲ You can make up other things to do when the car stops. Sing a song or say "Hooray" are fun to do too.

What your toddler will learn
▼
Concentration skills

▲▼▲▼▲▼▲▼▲▼▲▼▲▼▲▼▲▼▲▼▲▼▲▼▲▼▲▼▲

▲ outside games

Big Steps, Little Steps

▲▼▲▼▲▼▲▼▲▼▲▼▲▼▲▼▲▼▲▼▲▼▲▼▲▼▲▼▲

▲ Show your toddler that there is a variety of ways to walk. She can use large steps and tiny steps.

▲ Try walking around the yard with large steps.

▲ Now try walking across the yard with very tiny steps.

▲ Say this poem and do the actions.

Big step, big step, big step, big step

Tiny, tiny, tiny step

Big step

Big jump, big jump, big jump, big jump

Tiny, tiny, tiny jump

Big jump

Big run, big run, big run, big run

Tiny, tiny, tiny run

Big run

What your toddler will learn

▼

Coordination

▲▼▲▼▲▼▲▼▲▼▲▼▲▼▲▼▲▼▲▼▲▼▲▼▲▼▲▼▲

outside games ▲

Catch the Ball

▲▼▲▼▲▼▲▼▲▼▲▼▲▼▲▼▲▼▲▼▲▼▲▼▲▼▲▼

▲ Sit on the grass facing your toddler.

▲ Sit far enough apart that you can roll a ball to your toddler, and he can catch it easily.

▲ Encourage your child to roll the ball back to you.

▲ As your toddler gets good at doing this, make the rolling space wider between the two of you.

▲ Roll the ball to a tree or other outside place.

▲ Ask your toddler to bring it back to you or run with your toddler to get the ball.

What your toddler will learn

▼

Coordination

▲▼▲▼▲▼▲▼▲▼▲▼▲▼▲▼▲▼▲▼▲▼▲▼▲▼▲▼

▲ outside games

Bubbly Fun

▲ Fill a large bowl with water and place it on a table outside.

▲ Take a straw and blow gently on your child's hand.

▲ Show her how to take the straw and blow gently in the water.
Tip: Some children will need additional practice blowing OUT and not IN.
To prevent children from sucking up the water if they inhale, cut a V-shape
slit in the straw (about three inches from the top of the straw).

▲ Call her attention to the bubbles in the water.

▲ Once she gets the idea she will figure out that the harder she blows out,
the more bubbles she will have.

▲ Blowing is an important developmental skill for speech. The letters "p,"
"b" and "w" are all formed with a blowing motion.

▲ You can add detergent to the water for big, blowy bubbles if you desire.
Note: Add detergent only when your toddler understands that she should
only blow OUT and not IN.

What your toddler will learn
▼
Language skills

outside games ▲

Walk All Around

▲▼▲▼▲▼▲▼▲▼▲▼▲▼▲▼▲▼▲▼▲▼▲▼▲▼▲

▲ Do the following actions as you say the words. Encourage your toddler to copy you.

> *Walk all around,*
>
> *Walk all around,*
>
> *Run to the tree,*
>
> *Walk all around.*

▲ Keep saying the rhyme over and over with a different action. Always keep the words "run to the tree" the same.

▲ Suggestion include:

> *Jump up and down*
>
> *Tap on the ground*
>
> *Don't make a sound*

What your toddler will learn

▼

To follow directions

▲▼▲▼▲▼▲▼▲▼▲▼▲▼▲▼▲▼▲▼▲▼▲▼▲▼▲

▲ outside games

Quiet Games

▲▽▲▽▲▽▲▽▲▽▲▽▲▽▲▽▲▽▲▽▲▽▲▽▲▽▲▽▲▽▲▽▲▽▲

▲▽▲▽▲▽▲▽▲▽▲▽▲▽▲▽▲▽▲▽▲▽▲▽▲▽▲▽▲▽▲▽▲▽▲

Pat Your Head

▲ Hold your child in your arms. Pat your toddler's head three times and as you pat, say the words, "Pat, pat, pat."

▲ Take your toddler's hand and put it on your head. Show him how to pat your head.

▲ Repeat the same activity patting on the tummy and patting on the knee.

▲ Guide his hands as you say the following.

> *Pat your head, pat, pat, pat*
>
> *Pat my head, pat, pat, pat*
>
> *Where's your tummy? Pat, pat, pat*
>
> *Where's my tummy? Pat, pat, pat*
>
> *Pat your head, pat, pat, pat*
>
> *Pat my head, pat, pat, pat.*

> *Pat your head, pat, pat, pat*
>
> *Pat my head, pat, pat, pat*
>
> *Where's your knee? pat, pat, pat*
>
> *Where's my knee? pat, pat, pat*
>
> *Pat your head, pat, pat, pat*
>
> *Pat my head, pat, pat, pat.*

▲ When your child can identify these three body parts, add new ones.

What your toddler will learn

▼

About parts of the body

quiet games ▲

Wake Up

▲▼▲▼▲▼▲▼▲▼▲▼▲▼▲▼▲▼▲▼▲▼▲▼▲▼▲▼▲

▲ Greeting your toddler in the morning can be a wonderful bonding experience.

▲ Before you take him out of the crib, sing this song to the tune of "Ring Around the Rosy."

> *How are you this morning?*
>
> *How are you this morning?*
>
> *Wake up, wake up*
>
> *Open up your eyes. (touch your toddler's eyebrows)*

> *How are you this morning?*
>
> *How are you this morning?*
>
> *Wake up, wake up*
>
> *Stretch out your arms. (stretch your toddler's arms)*
>
> *Open up your eyes. (touch your toddler's eyebrows)*

▲ Keep singing the song and adding a new line each time. Always repeat the preceding lines.

> *Stretch your hands and toes*
>
> *Stretch your arms and feet*
>
> *Stretch your little neck*
>
> *Give me a kiss (pick up your child and kiss him)*

What your toddler will learn
▼
Bonding

▲▼▲▼▲▼▲▼▲▼▲▼▲▼▲▼▲▼▲▼▲▼▲▼▲▼▲▼▲

▲ quiet games

Dump the Balls

▲▼▲▼▲▼▲▼▲▼▲▼▲▼▲▼▲▼▲▼▲▼▲▼▲▼▲

▲ Place soft balls or other small soft objects in a box.

▲ Dump all of the balls out of the box.

▲ Encourage your child to pick up the balls one at a time and put them back into the box.

▲ Dump the balls out again and ask your child to pick them up.

▲ After you have played this game a few times, start dumping the balls out in different ways. For example, take them out one by one or tip the box over with your foot.

▲ Your child will quickly scramble to put the balls back into the box.

▲ Toddlers are absolutely delighted with this game and will soon be playing the game themselves.

What your toddler will learn
▼
Fine motor skills

quiet games ▲

To the Woods

▲▼▲▼▲▼▲▼▲▼▲▼▲▼▲▼▲▼▲▼▲▼▲▼▲▼▲▼▲▼

▲ This is a toe drying song. After a bath, one toe is dried for each line of the rhyme.

▲ On the last line hold your child and give her lots of hugs and kisses.

> *Let's go to the woods, says this pig*
>
> *What shall we do there, says this pig*
>
> *Look for our mommy, says this pig*
>
> *What shall we do with her, says this pig*
>
> *Give her lots of kisses, says this pig.*

What your toddler will learn

▼

Fun

▲▼▲▼▲▼▲▼▲▼▲▼▲▼▲▼▲▼▲▼▲▼▲▼▲▼▲▼▲▼

▲ quiet games

nighttime

▲ Establishing a bedtime routine is very important for a toddler. It gives her a sense of trust and stability.

▲ Rubbing her back and singing to her are nice ways to relax your energetic toddler who has been running and jumping all day.

▲ Sing the following to the tune of "Are You Sleeping." Rub your child's back at the same time.

> *Good night, Sarah. (substitute your toddler's name)*
>
> *Good night, Sarah.*
>
> *Go to sleep, go to sleep.*
>
> *Soon you will be dreaming,*
>
> *Soon you will be dreaming.*
>
> *I love you, I love you.*

What your toddler will learn

▼

Relaxation

quiet games ▲

Learning Opposites

▲▼▲▼▲▼▲▼▲▼▲▼▲▼▲▼▲▼▲▼▲▼▲▼▲▼▲▼▲▼

▲ Here are things that you can do to teach your toddler about opposites.

Swing him high in the air and say "high."

Swing him low to the ground and say "low."

Hold your toddlers arms and move them out and say "out."

Move his arms in and say "in."

Say "up" and "down" as you move his arms and legs up and down.

Drop an object in a container and say "in."

Take the object out and say "out."

What your toddler will learn

▼

About opposites

▲▼▲▼▲▼▲▼▲▼▲▼▲▼▲▼▲▼▲▼▲▼▲▼▲▼▲▼▲▼

▲ quiet games

Circle 'Round the Tummy

▲▼▲▼▲▼▲▼▲▼▲▼▲▼▲▼▲▼▲▼▲▼▲▼▲▼▲▼

▲ Lay your toddler on his back.

▲ Take your finger and trace a circle on his tummy.

▲ As you are making a circle on his tummy, sing the following song to the tune of "Ring Around the Rosy."

> *Circle 'round the tummy*
>
> *Circle 'round the tummy*
>
> *Faster, faster*
>
> *One, two tickle! (tickle your child's tummy)*

▲ Play this game on different parts of your toddler's body. His palm, his head and his back are good places to begin.

What your toddler will learn

▼

Bonding

quiet games ▲

Good Night, Sleep Tight

▲▼▲▼▲▼▲▼▲▼▲▼▲▼▲▼▲▼▲▼▲▼▲▼▲▼▲▼▲▼▲

▲ This is a nice rhyme to say to your toddler before you put him to bed.

▲ It's a good idea to say the same rhyme each night. Toddlers love consistency.

> *Good night, sleep tight*
>
> *Don't let the bedbugs bite.*
>
> *If they bite,*
>
> *Squeeze them tight.*
>
> *Good night, sleep tight.*

What your toddler will learn
▼
Bonding

▲▼▲▼▲▼▲▼▲▼▲▼▲▼▲▼▲▼▲▼▲▼▲▼▲▼▲▼▲▼▲

▲ quiet games

Chook, Chook

▲▼▲▼▲▼▲▼▲▼▲▼▲▼▲▼▲▼▲▼▲▼▲▼▲▼▲

▲ This is a wonderful fingerplay that will develop your child's fine motor skills and provide fun for you and your child.

▲ Sit your toddler in your lap and move his fingers to fit the rhyme.

> *Chook, chook*
>
> *Chook, chook, chook*
>
> *Good morning, Mrs. Hen*
>
> *How many chickens have you got?*
>
> *Madam, I've got ten.*
>
> *Four of them are yellow,*
>
> *And four of them are brown,*
>
> *And two of them are speckled red*
>
> *The nicest in the town.*

What your toddler will learn

▼

Fine motor skills

▲▼▲▼▲▼▲▼▲▼▲▼▲▼▲▼▲▼▲▼▲▼▲▼▲

quiet games ▲

The Tissue Game

▲▽▲▽▲▽▲▽▲▽▲▽▲▽▲▽▲▽▲▽▲▽▲▽▲▽▲▽▲▽▲

▲ Take a tissue box with 15 or 20 tissues left.

▲ Give it to your toddler and let her pull out the tissues. This is great fun for your child.

▲ Take the tissues that have been pulled from the box and show your child how to roll them into balls.

▲ Play silly games with the tissue balls. For example, put a ball on your head and let it fall off. Do the same with your toddler.

▲ Put as many tissue balls as you can in your hand and close it up tight. Say, "Abracadabra" and open your hand so the balls can fall out.

▲ Be prepared for lots of giggles.

What your toddler will learn
▼
Fine motor skills

▲▽▲▽▲▽▲▽▲▽▲▽▲▽▲▽▲▽▲▽▲▽▲▽▲▽▲▽▲▽▲

▲ quiet games

Five Little Kittens

▲▼▲▼▲▼▲▼▲▼▲▼▲▼▲▼▲▼▲▼▲▼▲▼▲▼▲

▲ Talk about kittens with your toddler. Make a "meow" sound and see if your child will imitate you.

▲ Whisper this rhyme about kittens.

> *Five little kittens (hold up five fingers)*
>
> *All black and white*
>
> *Sleeping very soundly*
>
> *All through the night. (make your hand into a fist)*
>
> *Meow, meow, meow, meow, meow,*
>
> *It's time to get up now. (raise one finger at a time as you say "meow")*

What your toddler will learn

▼

Language skills

▲▼▲▼▲▼▲▼▲▼▲▼▲▼▲▼▲▼▲▼▲▼▲▼▲▼▲

Which One?

▲ Put a dish towel on the floor and while your toddler is watching, hide a toy under the towel.

▲ Say, "Where is the toy? Can you find it?"

▲ When he finds the toy, praise him.

▲ Add a second towel and put the toy under the same towel. When your child starts to look for it, move the toy and put it under the second towel. Help him to find the toy under the second towel.

▲ Play this a few times and then add a third towel.

▲ Soon your toddler will look under all three towels to find the toy.

What your toddler will learn
▼
Thinking skills

Shoes for Fun

▲▼▲▼▲▼▲▼▲▼▲▼▲▼▲▼▲▼▲▼▲▼▲▼▲▼▲

▲ Take several pairs of shoes that belong to members of your family and put them together in a pile on the floor.

▲ As you put the shoes down, tell your toddler who they belong to.

▲ He will recognize his own shoes and will probably respond when he sees them.

▲ Now play the game by asking your child to bring you a particular pair of shoes. "Please bring me daddy's shoes."

▲ If he doesn't understand, go over to the pile and pick up one of daddy's shoes.

▲ Not only does this game develop thinking skills but it also is a hands-on experience in size comparison.

What your toddler will learn
▼
Thinking skills

▲▼▲▼▲▼▲▼▲▼▲▼▲▼▲▼▲▼▲▼▲▼▲▼▲▼▲

quiet games ▲

Hard and Soft

▲▼▲▼▲▼▲▼▲▼▲▼▲▼▲▼▲▼▲▼▲▼▲▼▲▼▲

▲ Tactile stimulation is a very important part of a child's development. By understanding how things feel, young children develop language and cognitive thinking.

▲ Toddlers can begin to understand if something is hard or soft.

▲ Give your toddler soft objects one at a time. Each time you give her an object, say the word "soft" in a soft gentle voice.

▲ Start with cotton balls, stuffed animals, pieces of soft material.

▲ Now give your toddler things to feel that are hard. Each time you give her the object, say the word "hard" in a different voice than the soft voice.

▲ A hard small toy or block are good to use.

▲ After you have played this game a few times, put a soft and a hard object in a paper sack. Let your child take one of the objects out of the sack and see if she can tell you if it is hard or soft.

What your toddler will learn
▼
About hard and soft

▲▼▲▼▲▼▲▼▲▼▲▼▲▼▲▼▲▼▲▼▲▼▲▼▲▼▲

Sticky Stuff

▲ Present your toddler with a variety of sticky things. Band-aids, stickers, tape, labels, etc.

▲ Give her a sticky something and ask her to put it on her knee.

▲ Then ask her to put it on her nose, then her hand and so on.

▲ This is great fun and it also helps teach about parts of the body.

▲ Play this game with all the members of the family.

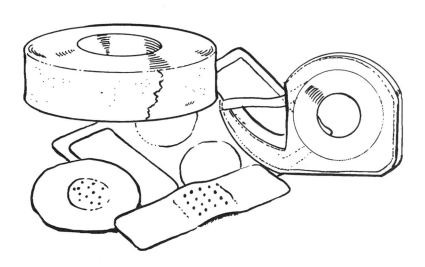

What your toddler will learn
▼
About parts of the body

quiet games ▲

First and Second

▲▼▲▼▲▼▲▼▲▼▲▼▲▼▲▼▲▼▲▼▲▼▲▼▲▼▲▼▲▼▲

▲ Understanding seriation—first, second, third—is a concept that develops after lots of hands-on play and language experience.

▲ Sit on the floor with your toddler. Show her a set of nesting measuring cups.

▲ Take them out one by one. As you take them out, say, "This is the first cup. This is the second cup." With young children first and second are enough.

▲ After your child has played with the cups for awhile, ask her to give you the first cup. Then ask her to give you the second cup.

▲ Repeat this game over and over always using the words "first" and "second."

What your toddler will learn
▼
About seriation

▲▼▲▼▲▼▲▼▲▼▲▼▲▼▲▼▲▼▲▼▲▼▲▼▲▼▲▼▲▼▲

▲ quiet games

Get the Toy

▲▼▲▼▲▼▲▼▲▼▲▼▲▼▲▼▲▼▲▼▲▼▲▼▲▼▲

▲ Find a plastic bottle with a lid. The lid should be small enough that your child can get his hand around it.

▲ Drop a small toy in the bottle and put the lid on. Don't turn it too tightly.

▲ Show your child how to turn the lid to get it off.

▲ Give the bottle to your toddler and let him take off the lid.

▲ After he has dumped out the toy, encourage him to put the toy back in the bottle.

▲ Play the game again.

▲ If your child begins to get bored, put a different toy or something to eat in the bottle.

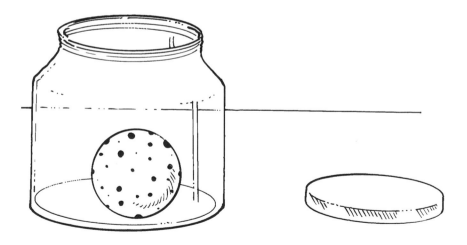

What your toddler will learn
▼
Coordination

▲▼▲▼▲▼▲▼▲▼▲▼▲▼▲▼▲▼▲▼▲▼▲▼▲▼▲

quiet games ▲

Wave to Your Mama

▲▼▲▼▲▼▲▼▲▼▲▼▲▼▲▼▲▼▲▼▲▼▲▼▲▼▲▼

▲ Say this rhyme as you shake your toddler's hands and feet.

▲ Start with the hands. Repeat the rhyme waving one hand at a time.

> *Wave to your mama,*
>
> *Wave to your mama*
>
> *My little babe.*
>
> *Wave to your papa,*
>
> *Wave to your papa*
>
> *My little babe.*
>
> *Jackie Silberg*

▲ Wave to different things in the room.

> *Wave to the window*
>
> *Wave to the door*
>
> *Wave to the teddy*

What your toddler will learn
▼
Coordination

▲ quiet games

Playing with Tongs

▲▼▲▼▲▼▲▼▲▼▲▼▲▼▲▼▲▼▲▼▲▼▲▼▲▼▲▼▲

▲ Present your toddler with two unbreakable bowls and a pair of tongs.

▲ Fill one bowl with cotton balls.

▲ Show your child how to use the tongs to move the cotton balls from one bowl into another.

▲ Your toddler will be fascinated and will spend a lot of time transferring the cotton balls from one container to the other.

▲ To extend this activity, pretend that you are having dinner.

▲ Ask your child, "Would you please serve the chicken?"

▲ When he moves one cotton ball to the other container, respond with, "Thank you, that looks delicious."

What your toddler will learn
▼
Fine motor skills

quiet games ▲

The Raisin Game

▲▼▲▼▲▼▲▼▲▼▲▼▲▼▲▼▲▼▲▼▲▼▲▼▲▼▲▼▲▼▲

▲ Raisins are a nutritious food and make great objects for fine motor skill development.

▲ Fill a small plastic bowl with raisins.

▲ Next to the bowl place a plastic jar with a lid. Be sure that the lid is loose so that your child will be able to remove it easily.

▲ Ask your toddler to put a raisin in the jar. In order for her to do this, she will have to remove the lid.

▲ After she has transferred all of the raisins to the jar, she can dump them out and start again.

▲ A young child can work at an activity like this for a long time.

What your toddler will learn

▼

Fine motor skills

▲▼▲▼▲▼▲▼▲▼▲▼▲▼▲▼▲▼▲▼▲▼▲▼▲▼▲▼▲▼▲

▲ quiet games

An Action Game

▲▼▲▼▲▼▲▼▲▼▲▼▲▼▲▼▲▼▲▼▲▼▲▼▲▼▲▼▲

▲ Say the following rhyme with your toddler and help him do the actions.

Here's a ball for (child's name) (form a ball with your arms)

Big and soft and round.

Here is (child's name) hammer

My how it can pound. (pound your fist)

Here is (child's name)

Toot-a-toot-a-toot. (blow a trumpet)

Here's how (child's name) plays

Peek-a, peek-a, boo. (hide your eyes)

Here's a big umbrella

Keeping (child's name) dry. (pretend to hold up an umbrella)

Here is (child's name) cradle

Rock-a-baby bye. (rock your child in your arms)

What your child will learn
▼
Fine motor skills

Foot Pats

▲▼▲▼▲▼▲▼▲▼▲▼▲▼▲▼▲▼▲▼▲▼▲▼▲▼▲▼▲▼▲

▲ Pat the soles of your toddler's feet as you say the following rhymes.

▲ These rhymes are nice to do at bedtime.

Pitty, patty, polt
Shoe the wild colt.
Here's a nail,
There's a nail,
Pitty, patty, polt.

Robert Barnes, fellow fine
Can you shoe this horse of mine?
Yes, good sir, that I can
As well as any other man.
There's a nail, and there's a prod,
And now, good sir, your horse is shod.

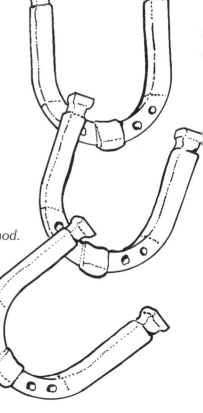

What your toddler will learn

▼

Fun

▲▼▲▼▲▼▲▼▲▼▲▼▲▼▲▼▲▼▲▼▲▼▲▼▲▼▲▼▲▼▲

▲ quiet games

Listening for the Sounds

▲▼▲▼▲▼▲▼▲▼▲▼▲▼▲▼▲▼▲▼▲▼▲▼▲▼▲▼▲

▲ Developing good listening skills helps your child with language and reading skills.

▲ There are so many sounds around us and it is important to help your child distinguish one sound from another.

▲ Start with the sounds around your house. A clock ticking, a musical toy or the sound of a bird chirping.

▲ Make your child aware of the sounds and even try to make the sounds that you hear.

▲ After you have talked about sounds for a while, begin asking your toddler to point to the sounds that you hear.

What your toddler will learn
▼
Listening skills

▲▼▲▼▲▼▲▼▲▼▲▼▲▼▲▼▲▼▲▼▲▼▲▼▲▼▲▼▲

quiet games ▲

Sensory Experiences

▲▼▲▼▲▼▲▼▲▼▲▼▲▼▲▼▲▼▲▼▲▼▲▼▲▼▲▼▲

▲ Your toddler loves to explore. Encourage her by taking her hand and touching many things. Materials of silk, wool, cotton and corduroy are a wonderful variety of touches.

▲ Help her compare how things feel by saying things such as, "This feels smooth and this feels silky."

▲ Nature provides wonderful smells (flowers, grass, leaves) as well as crunchy leaves to touch and soft grass to walk on.

▲ The kitchen is full of wonderful tastes—sweet, sour, spicy, etc.

▲ The supermarket is an excellent place for touching. Each time you put something in the shopping cart let your toddler touch the item.

What your toddler will learn
▼
About the senses

▲▼▲▼▲▼▲▼▲▼▲▼▲▼▲▼▲▼▲▼▲▼▲▼▲▼▲▼▲

▲ quiet games

Undressing

▲▼▲▼▲▼▲▼▲▼▲▼▲▼▲▼▲▼▲▼▲▼▲▼▲▼▲

▲ Toddlers can get very frustrated when they are trying to take off their shoes, socks, shirts, etc.

▲ There are many ways that you can help your toddler feel confident.

▲ If the shoes have laces, untie them. Loosen the lacing and pull the shoe over his heel. This enables him to take it off himself.

▲ If he is wearing a shirt, help him take off one sleeve and show him how to pull off the other one.

▲ Slip his socks over his heels so that he can pull off the sock.

▲ Your child will feel confident about being able to undress himself.

What your toddler will learn

▼

Confidence

▲▼▲▼▲▼▲▼▲▼▲▼▲▼▲▼▲▼▲▼▲▼▲▼▲▼▲

quiet games ▲

One, Two, Surprise!

▲▼▲▼▲▼▲▼▲▼▲▼▲▼▲▼▲▼▲▼▲▼▲▼▲▼▲▼▲

▲ Take a metal adhesive bandage box and show your child how to open the box and close it.

▲ Give the box to your child and let him open and close the box.

▲ Put a small toy or something that will rattle inside the box.

▲ Ask your toddler, "What is in the box?"

▲ Play a guessing game with the bandage box. Show an object to your toddler, then put it into the box. Ask, "What is in the box?"

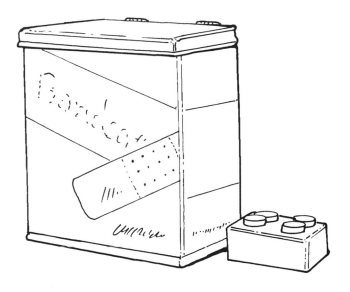

What your toddler will learn
▼
Fine motor skills

▲▼▲▼▲▼▲▼▲▼▲▼▲▼▲▼▲▼▲▼▲▼▲▼▲▼▲▼▲

▲ quiet games

Double Fun

▲ This game takes a lot of concentration for your toddler and will develop her thinking skills.

▲ Cut out a magazine picture that is something your child recognizes, for example, a piece of fruit.

▲ If you cut out a picture of a banana, put it on the floor in front of your toddler.

▲ Say, "Look at this picture of a banana. Yum, Yum."

▲ Talk about the picture with your child.

▲ Now, get a real banana and put it next to the picture.

▲ Talk about the real banana in the same way that you talked about the picture.

▲ Continue playing this game of matching the magazine picture to the real thing.

▲ Cut out several familiar objects and ask your child to take the picture and put it on the real object.

▲ For example, "Can you take this picture of the pillow and put it on the pillow?"

What your toddler will learn
▼
Thinking skills

quiet games ▲

Rhyming Games

Thread the Needle

▲▼▲▼▲▼▲▼▲▼▲▼▲▼▲▼▲▼▲▼▲▼▲▼▲▼▲▼▲

▲ Sit your toddler in your lap. On the words "thread the needle" and clap your child's hands together gently.

▲ On the words that describe a part of the body, take your child's hand and put it on that part of the body.

> *Thread the needle, thread the needle,*
>
> *Eye, eye, eye.*
>
> *Thread the needle, thread the needle,*
>
> *Eye, eye, eye.*
>
> *Thread the needle, thread the needle,*
>
> *Nose, nose, nose.*
>
> *Thread the needle, thread the needle,*
>
> *Nose, nose, nose.*

▲ Continue with different parts of the body.

What your toddler will learn
▼
About parts of the body

rhyming games ▲

Tickle Ickle

▲▼▲▼▲▼▲▼▲▼▲▼▲▼▲▼▲▼▲▼▲▼▲▼▲▼▲▼▲

▲ Hold your toddler in your arms and say the following rhyme.

Tickle, ickle, ickle

Little, little pickle.

Here's a little tickle

Tick, tick, tick. (tickle your toddler on the nose)

Tickle, ickle, ickle

Little, little chicken.

Have a little chuckle,

Chuck, chuck, chuck. (tickle your toddler on a different part of his body)

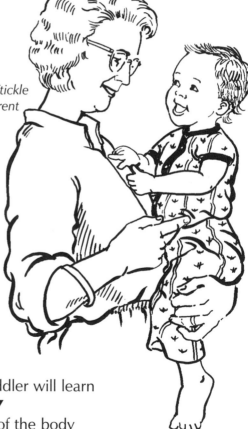

What your toddler will learn

▼

About parts of the body

▲ rhyming games

Roly Poly

▲ This is a great family game. When everybody is participating it makes it even more fun for your toddler.

▲ At the beginning hold your toddler's arms and move them accordingly. Soon he will be doing it all by himself.

Roly poly, roly poly (roll one fist over the other)

Up, up, up. (hold your arms up in the air)

Roly poly, roly poly (roll fists again)

Down, down, down. (hold arms down to the sides)

Roly poly, roly poly (roll fists again)

Out, out, out. (hold arms straight out to the sides)

Roly poly, roly poly (roll fists)

In, in, in. (bring arms in to your chest)

What your toddler will learn

▼

About spatial concepts

Mary Muffet

▲▼▲▼▲▼▲▼▲▼▲▼▲▼▲▼▲▼▲▼▲▼▲▼▲▼▲▼▲

▲ This is a great diaper changing game.

▲ With your toddler on her back, say the following English rhyme and do the actions.

> Knees up, Mary Muffet. (bend your child's knee)
>
> Knees up, Mary Brown. (bend the other knee)
>
> Knees up, Mary Macaroni. (bend both knees at the same time)
>
> Take your mommy's (daddy's) hand, oh! (take your child's hands in yours)

▲ Repeat the rhyme and change the part of the body.

> Toes up...
>
> Fingers up...
>
> Arms up...
>
> Head up....

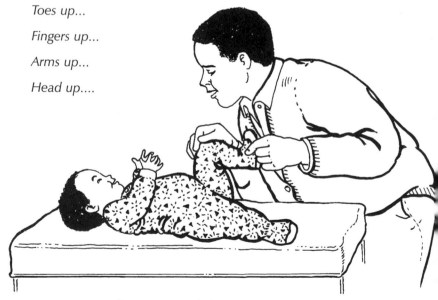

What your toddler will learn

▼

Bonding

▲▼▲▼▲▼▲▼▲▼▲▼▲▼▲▼▲▼▲▼▲▼▲▼▲▼▲▼▲

▲ rhyming games

Wee Wiggie

▲▼▲▼▲▼▲▼▲▼▲▼▲▼▲▼▲▼▲▼▲▼▲▼▲▼▲

▲ This is a toe tickling game.

▲ Touch each toe one at a time as you say each line starting with the big toe.

▲ When you come to the "gobble" part, run your fingers up your child's leg and tickle her tummy.

> Wee wiggie,
>
> Poke piggie,
>
> Tom whistle,
>
> John gristle,
>
> And old big gobble, gobble, gobble!

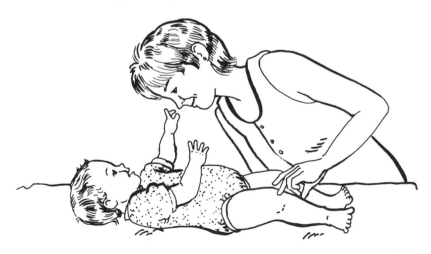

What your toddler will learn

Bonding

▲▼▲▼▲▼▲▼▲▼▲▼▲▼▲▼▲▼▲▼▲▼▲▼▲▼▲

rhyming games ▲

Arm Fun

▲▼▲▼▲▼▲▼▲▼▲▼▲▼▲▼▲▼▲▼▲▼▲▼▲▼▲▼▲

▲ Sit your baby in your lap and play the following game with her by saying the poem and doing the actions.

Put your arms up high, high, high. (lift up her arms)

Put your arms down low. (put her arms down)

Make your arms go stiff, stiff, stiff. (try to stiffen her arms)

Now you let them go. (try to relax her arms)

Swing your arms back and forth, (swing her arms)

Swing them just like that.

Make your arms go round and round, (roll her hands)

Now your arms are flat. (straighten out her arms)

What your toddler will learn
▼
Coordination

▲▼▲▼▲▼▲▼▲▼▲▼▲▼▲▼▲▼▲▼▲▼▲▼▲▼▲▼▲

▲ rhyming games

'Round About

▲▼▲▼▲▼▲▼▲▼▲▼▲▼▲▼▲▼▲▼▲▼▲▼▲▼▲

▲ Circle your finger around your toddler's palm. On the last line, creep up her arm and tickle her under the neck.

'Round about, 'round about

Catch a wee mouse.

Up a bit, up a bit

To her wee house.

'Round about, 'round about

Where did you roam?

Up a bit, up a bit

To my wee home.

What your toddler will learn

▼

Fun

▲▼▲▼▲▼▲▼▲▼▲▼▲▼▲▼▲▼▲▼▲▼▲▼▲▼▲

rhyming games ▲

The Cat's in the Tree

▲▼▲▼▲▼▲▼▲▼▲▼▲▼▲▼▲▼▲▼▲▼▲▼▲▼▲▼▲▼▲

▲ Play this game with your child sitting in your lap.

▲ Say the following rhyme.

> The cat's in the tree, (hold your child's arms up high in the air)
>
> Oh-oh, too high.
>
> The cat jumped down to the ground, (put your child's arms down)
>
> Oh-oh, too low.
>
> The cat jumped in your lap,
>
> Oh-oh, just right! (give your child a hug)
>
> Jackie Silberg

▲ Repeat the rhyme with different animals, toys, familiar people, etc. Your child will love saying the "oh-oh" part.

What your toddler will learn
▼
About high and low

▲▼▲▼▲▼▲▼▲▼▲▼▲▼▲▼▲▼▲▼▲▼▲▼▲▼▲▼▲▼▲

▲ rhyming games

Two Little Ears

▲▼▲▼▲▼▲▼▲▼▲▼▲▼▲▼▲▼▲▼▲▼▲▼▲▼▲

▲ Hold your toddler in your arms. Point to the specific body parts in the following rhyme as you say the words.

> *Two little ears for you to hear*
>
> *Two little eyes for you to see*
>
> *Two little lips for you to talk*
>
> *Sing along with me.*

> *La, la, la, (make up any melody)*
>
> *Two ears*
>
> *La, la, la,*
>
> *Two eyes*
>
> *La, la, la,*
>
> *Two lips*
>
> *You're my favorite _____(child's name). (give your child a big hug)*

What your toddler will learn

▼

About parts of the body

▲▼▲▼▲▼▲▼▲▼▲▼▲▼▲▼▲▼▲▼▲▼▲▼▲

　　　rhyming games ▲

Tiggoty Toggoty

▲▼▲▼▲▼▲▼▲▼▲▼▲▼▲▼▲▼▲▼▲▼▲▼▲▼▲▼▲▼▲

▲ Say the following rhyme with your child and have fun together.

Tiggoty, toggoty, gutter

Call the hogs to supper.

This one's fat, (tickle your child's left leg)

This one's lean, (tickle your child's right leg)

And this little hog is in between. (tickle your child's tummy)

What your toddler will learn

▼

Fun

▲▼▲▼▲▼▲▼▲▼▲▼▲▼▲▼▲▼▲▼▲▼▲▼▲▼▲▼▲▼▲

Chop a Nose

▲▼▲▼▲▼▲▼▲▼▲▼▲▼▲▼▲▼▲▼▲▼▲▼▲▼▲▼

▲ Hold your toddler's nose between the finger and thumb of one of your hands and "chop it off" with the other.

> *My mother and your mother*
> *Went over the way.*
> *My mother told your mother*
> *It's chop-a-nose day!*
>
> *My mother and your mother*
> *Went out to play.*
> *My mother told your mother*
> *It's chop-a-nose day!*

What your toddler will learn

▼

Fun

▲▼▲▼▲▼▲▼▲▼▲▼▲▼▲▼▲▼▲▼▲▼▲▼▲▼▲▼

rhyming games ▲

This Is the House

▲▼▲▼▲▼▲▼▲▼▲▼▲▼▲▼▲▼▲▼▲▼▲▼▲▼▲▼▲

▲ Say the following rhyme with your toddler and do the actions.

>   *This is the house where (child's name) lives.*
>
>   *This is the house where (child's name) lives. (touch the fingers of both hands together in an upward motion)*
>
>   *Where is (child's name)?*
>
>   *Here she is! (point to the child)*
>
>   *Here she is! (point to the child)*

▲ Repeat the poem naming other people or animals that live at your house.

▲ For example:

>   *This is the house where mommy lives...*
>
>   *This is the house where (dog's name) lives.*

What your toddler will learn

▼

Language skills

▲▼▲▼▲▼▲▼▲▼▲▼▲▼▲▼▲▼▲▼▲▼▲▼▲▼▲▼▲

▲ rhyming games

Sally Go 'Round the Sun

▲▼▲▼▲▼▲▼▲▼▲▼▲▼▲▼▲▼▲▼▲▼▲▼▲▼▲▼▲▼

▲ This is a lovely fingerplay that your toddler will want to play all of the time.

> *Sally go 'round the sun, (make a circle with your hands over your head and rock back and forth)*
>
> *Sally go 'round the moon.*
>
> *Sally go 'round the sunshine*
>
> *Every afternoon.*
>
> *Boom! Boom! (clap your hands over your head)*

▲ Repeat and clap on the "boom, boom" part in front of you.

▲ Keep clapping in different places.

What your toddler will learn
▼
Listening skills

▲▼▲▼▲▼▲▼▲▼▲▼▲▼▲▼▲▼▲▼▲▼▲▼▲▼▲▼▲▼

rhyming games ▲

Copy Me

▲▼▲▼▲▼▲▼▲▼▲▼▲▼▲▼▲▼▲▼▲▼▲▼▲▼▲▼▲

▲ Say the following rhyme with your toddler.

> *I put my hand on my head, (put your hand on your head)*
>
> *Copy me, copy me.*
>
> *Put your hand on your head, (guide your child's hand)*
>
> *Twiddle dee, twiddle dee, twiddle dee dee. (hold your child's hand and walk around in a circle)*
>
> Jackie Silberg

▲ Keep repeating the poem, and each time put your hand on a different part of the body.

▲ Soon your toddler will be able to place his hand on the correct part of the body without your help.

▲ On the "twiddle dee dee" part, you can do many things. Clap your hands, stamp your feet, jump up and down or give your child a hug.

What your toddler will learn

▼

Observation skills

▲ rhyming games

Blink Your Eyes

▲▼▲▼▲▼▲▼▲▼▲▼▲▼▲▼▲▼▲▼▲▼▲▼▲▼▲▼▲▼▲

▲ Say the following poem and do the actions as you say the words.

> *Blink your eyes,*
>
> *Blow a kiss with your lips,*
>
> *Move your shoulders,*
>
> *Put your hands on your hips.*
>
> *Wiggle your bottom,*
>
> *And wiggle your toes,*
>
> *Touch your ear,*
>
> *And touch your nose.*

▲ Say the poem again very slowly. With each action, encourage your child to copy you.

▲ When your toddler can do all of the actions, say the poem and let him do the actions by himself.

What your toddler will learn
▼
About parts of the body

rhyming games ▲

Rubby Dubby

▲▼▲▼▲▼▲▼▲▼▲▼▲▼▲▼▲▼▲▼▲▼▲▼▲▼▲▼▲▼▲

▲ This is a great bathtub game. Say the following rhyme as you bathe your baby with a wash cloth.

Rubby, dubby, rubby, dubby

Splash, splash, splash. (splash lightly with the wash cloth)

Rubby, dubby, rubby, dubby

Splash, splash, splash. (splash lightly with the wash cloth)

Where's your toe rubby dubby?

There it is rubby dubby!

Rubby, dubby, rubby, dubby (wash your child's toe)

Splash, splash, splash. (splash again)

Jackie Silberg

What your toddler will learn

▼

About parts of the body

▲▼▲▼▲▼▲▼▲▼▲▼▲▼▲▼▲▼▲▼▲▼▲▼▲▼▲▼▲▼▲

A Cat Poem

▲▼▲▼▲▼▲▼▲▼▲▼▲▼▲▼▲▼▲▼▲▼▲▼▲▼▲

▲ Sit your child on your lap.

▲ Take your fingers and run up and down his arm as you say the poem.

> *Diddlety, diddlety, dumpty,*
>
> *The cat ran up the plum tree.*
>
> *Half a crown*
>
> *To fetch her down,*
>
> *Diddlety, diddlety, dumpty.*

▲ Encourage your toddler to say the word diddlety. It makes the game even more fun when he tries to say the words.

What your toddler will learn
▼
Language skills

▲▼▲▼▲▼▲▼▲▼▲▼▲▼▲▼▲▼▲▼▲▼▲▼▲▼▲

rhyming games ▲

Someone Special

▲▽▲▽▲▽▲▽▲▽▲▽▲▽▲▽▲▽▲▽▲▽▲▽▲▽▲▽▲▽▲

▲ Say the following poem to your toddler.

I know someone very special.

Do you know who?

I'll turn around and turn around, (turn around)

And then I'll point to you! (point to your child)

Jackie Silberg

▲ Ask your child to turn around as you say the poem.

▲ Repeat the poem and each time instead of the words "turn around" change the action. You can jump up and down, clap your hands, fly like a bird, etc.

▲ Your child will need to listen to you in order to do the action that you say.

What your toddler will learn
▼
Listening skills

▲▽▲▽▲▽▲▽▲▽▲▽▲▽▲▽▲▽▲▽▲▽▲▽▲▽▲▽▲▽▲

▲ rhyming games

The Popcorn Game

▲▼▲▼▲▼▲▼▲▼▲▼▲▼▲▼▲▼▲▼▲▼▲▼▲▼▲

▲ Sit your toddler in your lap.

▲ Say the following rhyme.

> *I'm a piece of popcorn sitting in a pan.*
>
> *Shake me, shake me as fast as you can. (gently wiggle your toddler)*
>
> *Get ready...*
>
> *Pop! (as you say the word "pop" hold your child up high in the air)*

▲ Your toddler will anticipate the word "pop" and start laughing before you say it.

▲ This is a wonderful game to play in a swimming pool where the "pop" is combined with splashing.

What your toddler will learn
▼
Trust

▲▼▲▼▲▼▲▼▲▼▲▼▲▼▲▼▲▼▲▼▲▼▲▼▲▼▲

rhyming games ▲

One, Two, Buckle My Shoe

▲ This lovely nursery rhyme is fun to play with members of the family.

▲ One person counts and another person says the rhyme.

▲ Your toddler will not only hear the numbers but will see how everyone has fun together.

▲ Hold your toddler in your lap as you say the rhyme. After once or twice, your child will catch on and will begin saying the numbers while you say the rest of the rhyme.

> *One, two, buckle my shoe.*
>
> *Three, four, knock at the door.*
>
> *Five, six, pick up sticks.*
>
> *Seven, eight, lay them straight.*

▲ You can also act out the rhymes as they are said.

What your toddler will learn
▼
About counting

▲ rhyming games

Winding up the Clock

▲▼▲▼▲▼▲▼▲▼▲▼▲▼▲▼▲▼▲▼▲▼▲▼▲▼▲▼▲

▲ Show your toddler a wind-up clock.

▲ Show her how you can wind it up on the back. You could also use a stuffed animal that has a wind-up part.

▲ Let your toddler listen to the "tick tock" of the clock.

▲ Imitate the sound and say the words "tick tock."

▲ Play the following game.

> *Winding up the clock, (hold your child's hand and move her arm in a circle)*
>
> *Winding up the clock, (keep winding)*
>
> *Tick, tock, tick, tock, (move your head back and forth)*
>
> *Winding up the clock. (start winding again)*

What your toddler will learn
▼
Coordination

▲▼▲▼▲▼▲▼▲▼▲▼▲▼▲▼▲▼▲▼▲▼▲▼▲▼▲▼▲

rhyming games ▲

Tommy Thumb

▲▼▲▼▲▼▲▼▲▼▲▼▲▼▲▼▲▼▲▼▲▼▲▼▲▼▲▼

▲ Everyone in the family can play this variation of "Where Is Thumbkin?" The game is played by holding your hands behind your back, and bringing out each finger as it is called.

> *Tommy Thumb, Tommy Thumb*
>
> *Where are you?*
>
> *Here I am. (bring out one thumb)*
>
> *Here I am. (bring out the other thumb)*
>
> *How do you do. (wiggle each thumb toward the other thumb)*

▲ Repeat with:

> *Peter Pointer—forefinger*
>
> *Toby Tall—middle finger*
>
> *Ruby Ring—ring finger*
>
> *Baby Small—little finger*
>
> *Fingers all—all five fingers on each hand*

▲ Another variation:

> *Thumbkin says to dance. (show one thumb)*
>
> *Thumbkin says to sing. (show other thumb)*
>
> *Dance and sing you merry little thing. (wag thumbs towards each other)*
>
> *Thumbkin says to dance and sing. (keep wagging thumbs)*

▲ Repeat the same poem with each finger.

> *Pointer, Middle finger, Ring finger, Pinkie*

What your toddler will learn

▼

Fine motor skills

▲▼▲▼▲▼▲▼▲▼▲▼▲▼▲▼▲▼▲▼▲▼▲▼▲▼▲▼

What Did It Say?

▲▼▲▼▲▼▲▼▲▼▲▼▲▼▲▼▲▼▲▼▲▼▲▼▲▼▲

▲ Talk with your toddler about the sounds that animals make.

▲ Look at a book with animal pictures and encourage your child to make the animal sounds.

▲ Say this poem and let your child fill in the sounds.

> I went to visit the farm one day.
>
> I saw a cow across the way.
>
> What do you think I heard it say? (child says "Moo")

▲ Repeat the poem and name a different animal that your toddler knows.

▲ You can also make transportation sounds of cars, trains, airplanes.

M o o o o

What your toddler will learn

▼

Language skills

▲▼▲▼▲▼▲▼▲▼▲▼▲▼▲▼▲▼▲▼▲▼▲▼▲▼▲

rhyming games ▲

Who Is Tapping?

▲▼▲▼▲▼▲▼▲▼▲▼▲▼▲▼▲▼▲▼▲▼▲▼▲▼▲▼▲▼▲

▲ This rhyme is a lot of fun and not only teaches observation skills but also develops language skills.

▲ It's best to play this game when it is raining outside.

▲ Listen to the rain with your toddler. Make him aware of how it sounds as it falls on the roof and the windows.

> *Who is tapping at my window?*
>
> *"It's not I," said the mommy.*
>
> *"It's not I," said the daddy.*
>
> *"It's not I," said (child's name).*
>
> *"It's not I," said the chair.*
>
> *"It's not I," said the table. (keep naming familiar objects in the room)*

▲ Finally say:

> *"It is I," said the rain,*
>
> *Tapping on your windowpane.*

What your toddler will learn

▼

Observation skills

▲▼▲▼▲▼▲▼▲▼▲▼▲▼▲▼▲▼▲▼▲▼▲▼▲▼▲▼▲▼▲

Here Comes a Bluebird

▲▼▲▼▲▼▲▼▲▼▲▼▲▼▲▼▲▼▲▼▲▼▲▼▲▼▲▼▲▼▲

▲ Stand and face your toddler. Take his hands in yours.

▲ While holding hands, walk around in a circle and sing the following rhyme with your own melody.

> *Here comes a bluebird through the window*
>
> *Here comes a bluebird through the door*
>
> *Here comes a bluebird through the window*
>
> *Fly and touch the chair.*

▲ On the words "fly and touch the chair," pretend to fly to the chair. Ask your toddler to do the same thing.

▲ Each time that you sing this little rhyme, fly and touch something different.

▲ This game teaches vocabulary in a very pleasant way. To make the game a little more difficult, name objects to fly to that are in a different room.

What your toddler will learn

▼

Vocabulary

rhyming games ▲

Running & Jumping

▲▽▲▽▲▽▲▽▲▽▲▽▲▽▲▽▲▽▲▽▲▽▲▽▲▽▲▽▲▽▲

Games

▲▽▲▽▲▽▲▽▲▽▲▽▲▽▲▽▲▽▲▽▲▽▲▽▲▽▲▽▲▽▲

Balloon Fun

▲▼▲▼▲▼▲▼▲▼▲▼▲▼▲▼▲▼▲▼▲▼▲▼▲▼▲▼▲

▲ This game is very challenging to your toddler who is just learning to walk.

▲ Tie a few balloons to the end of a string and tape the end of the string to the ceiling. Do this in the middle of the room.

▲ The balloons should be hanging low enough that your toddler can reach them.

▲ Show your toddler how to hit at the balloons.

▲ Stand at the end of the room and say, "One, two, run to the balloons."

▲ Run to the balloons and bat them back and forth.

What your toddler will learn
▼
Coordination

▲▼▲▼▲▼▲▼▲▼▲▼▲▼▲▼▲▼▲▼▲▼▲▼▲▼▲▼▲

The Big Chase

▲ Toddlers love to chase things. If you put something movable on the floor, they will chase after it.

▲ Get on the floor with your toddler and say, "Chase me." Start crawling slowly to a specific place. When your toddler chases after you, praise her.

▲ Now that she has the idea, try crawling and hiding behind something. Be sure that she sees where you are hiding so that she can follow you.

▲ Crawl somewhere under an object like a table.

▲ Crawl into a different room.

▲ Think of all the places that you can crawl with your toddler chasing you. She will truly enjoy this game and develop her motor and spatial skills at the same time.

What your toddler will learn
▼
Coordination

Let's Roll!

▲▼▲▼▲▼▲▼▲▼▲▼▲▼▲▼▲▼▲▼▲▼▲▼▲▼▲

▲ Your toddler is in a constant state of motion. Crawling, climbing, walking, running, etc.

▲ Show your child how to roll. Lie down on the floor and roll from one end to the other. He will be delighted and will want to copy you.

▲ Play this game. Lie down on the floor side by side. Count to three. On the count of three, say in a big voice, "Let's Roll!" Start rolling to the other side of the room.

▲ Be prepared to play this game often.

What your toddler will learn
▼
Coordination

▲▼▲▼▲▼▲▼▲▼▲▼▲▼▲▼▲▼▲▼▲▼▲▼▲▼▲

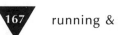

running & jumping games ▲

I Was

▲▼▲▼▲▼▲▼▲▼▲▼▲▼▲▼▲▼▲▼▲▼▲▼▲▼▲▼▲▼▲

▲ Sing the following song to the tune of "Mary Had a Little Lamb."

When I was a little girl (boy)

Little girl, little girl,

When I was a little girl

I could jump like this.

▲ Jump up and down and encourage your toddler to jump too.

▲ Sing the song again and change the action of the last line. Some different actions are turn, rock, kick, bend and run.

What your toddler will learn

▼

Coordination

▲▼▲▼▲▼▲▼▲▼▲▼▲▼▲▼▲▼▲▼▲▼▲▼▲▼▲▼▲▼▲

Jump, Jump, Kangaroo

▲▼▲▼▲▼▲▼▲▼▲▼▲▼▲▼▲▼▲▼▲▼▲▼▲▼▲

▲ If your child cannot jump, hold her at the waist and move her up and down.

▲ Every time the word "jump" is said, move your child up and down in a jumping motion.

>*Kangaroo, kangaroo, jump, jump, jump.*
>
>*Kangaroo, kangaroo, stop, stop, stop. (clap your hands)*
>
>*Kangaroo, kangaroo, jump up high.*
>
>*Kangaroo, kangaroo, jump to the sky.*
>
>*Kangaroo, kangaroo, go to sleep. (lie down on the floor and pretend to sleep)*
>
>*Good night.*

What your toddler will learn

▼

Coordination

▲▼▲▼▲▼▲▼▲▼▲▼▲▼▲▼▲▼▲▼▲▼▲▼▲▼▲

Hickory Dickory

▲▼▲▼▲▼▲▼▲▼▲▼▲▼▲▼▲▼▲▼▲▼▲▼▲▼▲▼

▲ Here is a different way to act out the popular nursery rhyme "Hickory, Dickory, Dock."

> *Hickory, dickory, dock (run around in a circle)*
>
> *The mouse ran up the clock.*
>
> *The clock struck one, (stop)*
>
> *And down he came, (fall down to the ground)*
>
> *Hickory, dickory, dock. (say cuckoo)*

What your toddler will learn

▼

Listening skills

▲▼▲▼▲▼▲▼▲▼▲▼▲▼▲▼▲▼▲▼▲▼▲▼▲▼▲▼

Cat and Mouse

▲ Tell your toddler that you are a tiny little mouse and that she is the cat that is going to chase you.

▲ Tell your toddler that the mouse says, "Squeak, squeak" and the cat says, "Meow, meow."

▲ Get down on the floor and say, "You can't catch me!" Start crawling fast and encourage your child to chase you.

▲ Crawl behind furniture, under tables and into other rooms.

▲ When your child understands the game, switch parts.

What your toddler will learn

▼

Observation skills

running & jumping games ▲

The Spinning Top

▲▼▲▼▲▼▲▼▲▼▲▼▲▼▲▼▲▼▲▼▲▼▲▼▲▼▲▼▲

▲ Show your child a top and let her watch it spin.

▲ Ask your child if she can spin like a top.

▲ Demonstrate how a top can spin and encourage her to try it.

▲ Say the following rhyme and spin like tops.

I'm a spinning top going round and round, (spin like a top)

And when I stop, I fall to the ground. (fall down to the ground)

▲ Once your toddler understands the game, try starting to spin slowly and get faster and faster. Then, start to slow down before you hit the ground.

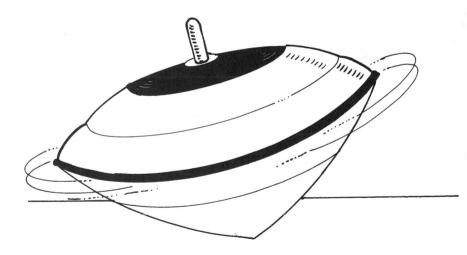

What your toddler will learn
▼
Coordination

▲▼▲▼▲▼▲▼▲▼▲▼▲▼▲▼▲▼▲▼▲▼▲▼▲▼▲▼▲

Can You Tell Me?

▲▼▲▼▲▼▲▼▲▼▲▼▲▼▲▼▲▼▲▼▲▼▲▼▲▼▲

▲ This game helps toddlers associate the language that goes with motor skills.

▲ Say to your toddler, "Can you tell me what I am doing?"

▲ Jump up and down a few times. Then say, "I am jumping."

▲ Now say to your child, "Can you jump like me?"

▲ Help your child jump up and down.

▲ Repeat this activity with several motor skills. Marching, swimming (use your arms) and running are all good ones.

What your toddler will learn

▼

Coordination

▲▼▲▼▲▼▲▼▲▼▲▼▲▼▲▼▲▼▲▼▲▼▲▼▲▼▲

Hi!

▲▽▲▽▲▽▲▽▲▽▲▽▲▽▲▽▲▽▲▽▲▽▲▽▲▽▲▽

▲ Say the following to your toddler.

> *Hi, said the elephant*
>
> *Can you see my trunk swing back and forth? (swing your arm in front of your face and walk slowly like an elephant)*
>
> *Hi, said the bunny*
>
> *Can you see my fluffy tail as I hop, hop, hop? (hop like a bunny)*

▲ On a table nearby have some peanuts and carrot sticks.

▲ Ask your toddler to join you and be an elephant. Walk like an elephant to the table to get the peanuts.

▲ Now hop to the table like a bunny to get the carrots.

▲ Now run to the table like a person to get your favorite treat.

What your toddler will learn

▼

Coordination

▲▽▲▽▲▽▲▽▲▽▲▽▲▽▲▽▲▽▲▽▲▽▲▽▲▽▲▽

What Can I Do?

▲▼▲▼▲▼▲▼▲▼▲▼▲▼▲▼▲▼▲▼▲▼▲▼▲▼▲▼▲

▲ Sing the following song to the tune of "What Shall We Do With a Drunken Sailor" and do the actions.

What can I do with both my feet,

What can I do with both my feet,

What can I do with both my feet,

Early in the morning?

Give a little clap and jump up and down,

Give a little clap and jump up and down,

Give a little clap and jump up and down,

Early in the morning.

▲ Continue with:

Give a little clap and run in a circle...

Give a little clap and hop up and down...

Give a little clap and shake my foot...

Give a little clap and shake my whole body...

▲ Make up your own verses.

What your toddler will learn

▼

Coordination

running & jumping games ▲

Where Can I Jump?

▲▼▲▼▲▼▲▼▲▼▲▼▲▼▲▼▲▼▲▼▲▼▲▼▲▼▲

▲ Toddlers can run and jump forever. Provide lots of opportunities for your child to exercise his muscles.

▲ Place barriers for your child to jump over. Start with something low and raise them higher. Blocks are good barriers for jumping.

▲ If your child has some trouble, help him by lifting him at the waist.

▲ Make a circle with masking tape and show your toddler how to jump in and out of the circle.

▲ Outside, encourage you child to jump off curbs and over water puddles.

▲ Pretend to be a kangaroo and jump everywhere.

What your toddler will learn

▼

Coordination

▲▼▲▼▲▼▲▼▲▼▲▼▲▼▲▼▲▼▲▼▲▼▲▼▲▼▲

▲ running & jumping games 176

I've Got a Body

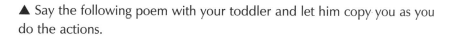

▲ Say the following poem with your toddler and let him copy you as you do the actions.

I've got a body that goes everywhere with me.

On my body is a nose that goes everywhere with me.

Sniff, sniff, here

Sniff, sniff, there

Sniff, sniff, sniff, sniff, everywhere

I've got a body that goes everywhere with me.

▲ Repeat the first two lines changing the word "nose" to another body part and then do the appropriate action.

...hands...clap...

...feet...stamp...

...feet...jump...

...throat...yell...

...fingers...wiggle...

What your toddler will learn

▼

Coordination

Have a Happy Day

▲▼▲▼▲▼▲▼▲▼▲▼▲▼▲▼▲▼▲▼▲▼▲▼▲▼▲▼▲▼▲

▲ Hold your toddler's hands and walk around in a circle.

▲ As you walk, sing the following song to the tune of "Mary Had a Little Lamb."

> *Have a happy day, today,*
>
> *Day, today,*
>
> *Day, today.*
>
> *Have a happy day, today,*
>
> *Clap your hands like me.*

▲ Sing the song many times and change the last line to a different activity.

> *Stamp your feet like me*
>
> *Turn around like me*
>
> *Touch your toes like me*

What your toddler will learn

▼

Coordination

▲▼▲▼▲▼▲▼▲▼▲▼▲▼▲▼▲▼▲▼▲▼▲▼▲▼▲▼▲▼▲

▲ running & jumping games 178

Shoe a Little Horse

▲▼▲▼▲▼▲▼▲▼▲▼▲▼▲▼▲▼▲▼▲▼▲▼▲▼▲▼▲▼▲

▲ Take off your shoes and ask your toddler to do the same.

▲ Say the following rhyme and do the actions with your toddler.

> Shoe a little horse. *(tap the bottom of your child's foot)*
>
> Shoe a little mare. *(keep tapping)*
>
> But let the little colt run bare, bare, bare.

▲ On the words "bare, bare, bare," run in place as fast as you can.

▲ After you have played this a few times, encourage your child to play the game with one of her stuffed animals. You say the words and let her play the game.

What your toddler will learn
▼
Fun

▲▼▲▼▲▼. .▼▲▼. .▼. .▼. .▼▲▼. .▼▲▼▲▼. .▼▲▼. .▼▲▼. .▼▲

Cows in the Meadow

▲▽▲▽▲▽▲▽▲▽▲▽▲▽▲▽▲▽▲▽▲▽▲▽▲▽▲▽▲

▲ Toddlers love this game because they can be very quiet and then very noisy.

▲ Ask your child to pretend to be a cow. Walk around the room saying, "Moo, moo."

▲ Now say the following poem and do the actions.

> *Cows in the meadow (say, "Moo, moo")*
>
> *Take a little nap. (put your head on your hands as if to go to sleep)*
>
> *Thunder, (stamp on the floor)*
>
> *Lightening, (put your hands up high to the sky)*
>
> *Jump up and clap. (jump up and down and clap hard)*

What your toddler will learn
▼
Listening skills

▲▽▲▽▲▽▲▽▲▽▲▽▲▽▲▽▲▽▲▽▲▽▲▽▲▽▲▽▲

▲ running & jumping games

Look at Yourself

▲▼▲▼▲▼▲▼▲▼▲▼▲▼▲▼▲▼▲▼▲▼▲▼▲▼▲

▲ This is a wonderful game to help your child learn about the different parts of his body.

▲ Say to your toddler, "If you are wearing shoes, jump up and down."

▲ Help your child by pointing to his shoes and saying, "Look, you have on shoes. Now you can jump up and down."

▲ Follow each instruction by pointing to that part of his body and showing him how to do the actions.

▲ Here are other ideas.

If you are wearing a belt, twist back and forth.

If you are wearing a shirt, clap your hands.

If you are wearing a hat, shake your head up and down.

▲ Once you have played this game a few times, you will find that your child can do the actions without your help.

What your toddler will learn
▼
Listening skills

▲▼▲▼▲▼▲▼▲▼▲▼▲▼▲▼▲▼▲▼▲▼▲▼▲▼▲

Seasonal Games

Snowflakes

▲▼▲▼▲▼▲▼▲▼▲▼▲▼▲▼▲▼▲▼▲▼▲▼▲▼▲▼▲▼

▲ Snowflakes are beautiful to watch and feel wonderful on the skin.

▲ If you live in an area that has snow, take your toddler outside when the snow is falling.

▲ Talk about how the snow feels on your face. Use words like "cool," "gentle" and "soft."

▲ Try to catch a snowflake.

▲ Fold a piece of white paper in half, in half again and in half again. Cut zig zags along the fold. When you open up the paper, you will have a snowflake.

▲ Make a snowflake mobile by cutting snowflakes out of paper and attaching them to a wire hanger.

What your toddler will learn

▼

About nature

▲▼▲▼▲▼▲▼▲▼▲▼▲▼▲▼▲▼▲▼▲▼▲▼▲▼▲▼▲▼

Smells

▲▼▲▼▲▼▲▼▲▼▲▼▲▼▲▼▲▼▲▼▲▼▲▼▲▼▲

▲ Your toddler had a fully developed sense of smell at birth. You may have memories associated with smells.

▲ Play a smell game with your child. Think of several objects with easily identifiable smells, such as flowers or grass.

▲ The kitchen is full of wonderful odors especially spices.

▲ Say to your child, "Let's smell the flowers." Hold a flower up to his nose and show him how to smell it.

▲ Respond to the smell with, "Oh, that smells wonderful."

▲ After you have smelled two things (for example cinnamon and flowers), put a flower and some cinnamon on a table. Ask your child to point to the flower. Help him point if he doesn't know how and then smell it together.

▲ Repeat the same thing with the cinnamon.

▲ Take advantage of the season to smell things in the outdoors.

What your toddler will learn
▼
About the sense of smell

▲ seasonal games

Blow, Wind, Blow

▲▼▲▼▲▼▲▼▲▼▲▼▲▼▲▼▲▼▲▼▲▼▲▼▲▼▲

▲ Listen to the wind and help your toddler become aware of the sound.

▲ Go outside and watch how the wind moves things like grass, branches and leaves.

▲ Show your toddler how to blow with his lips.

▲ Show him how to hold his hand in front of his mouth and blow on his hand.

▲ When he understands how to blow with his lips, say the following poem.

> *Blow, wind, blow*
>
> *Blow on my nose*
>
> *Blow, blow, blow on my nose. (blow on your child's nose)*

▲ Now ask your toddler to blow on your nose.

▲ Continue the poem and blow on another part of the body.

> *Blow, wind, blow*
>
> *Blow on my fingers*
>
> *Blow, blow, on my fingers.*

▲ Keep changing the part of the body.

What your toddler will learn

▼

About blowing

▲▼▲▼▲▼▲▼▲▼▲▼▲▼▲▼▲▼▲▼▲▼▲▼▲▼▲

seasonal games ▲

A Spring Day

▽▲▽▲▽▲▽▲▽▲▽▲▽▲▽▲▽▲▽▲▽▲▽▲▽▲▽▲▽▲▽▲▽▲

▲ Take your toddler outside on a wonderful spring day and enjoy the beauty and the smells of nature.

▲ Dance around and say the following rhyme as you hold your child in your arms.

> Come let's sing and dance in a ring
>
> Say hello to spring.
>
> "Hello spring, hello spring"
>
> Say hello to spring.

▲ Walk around and point out the signs of spring. Show your toddler the new grass and say, "Hello, grass."

▲ Show your toddler the flowers peeping out of the ground and say, "Hello, flowers."

▲ Look for all the signs of spring and say "hello" to them.

What your toddler will learn
▼
About nature

▲▽▲▽▲▽▲▽▲▽▲▽▲▽▲▽▲▽▲▽▲▽▲▽▲▽▲▽▲▽▲▽▲▽▲

▲ seasonal games

Rainy Days

▲▼▲▼▲▼▲▼▲▼▲▼▲▼▲▼▲▼▲▼▲▼▲▼▲▼▲▼▲

▲ Show your toddler how to take her hands and move them back and forth like a windshield wiper.

▲ As you move her hands back and forth, say the words "Swish, swish."

▲ Put her palm against your palm on each hand. Make the windshield wiper go slowly, and then faster and faster.

▲ With your palms together, say the following rhyme.

> Windshield wiper, windshield wiper
>
> What do you do all day?
>
> Swish, swish, swish, swish
>
> I wipe the rain away.
>
> Windshield wiper, windshield wiper
>
> Do you ever stop?
>
> Swish, swish, swish, swish
>
> When the rain goes away.

▲ This is a good game to play on a rainy day.

What your toddler will learn
▼
Coordination

▲▼▲▼▲▼▲▼▲▼▲▼▲▼▲▼▲▼▲▼▲▼▲▼▲▼▲▼▲

Where Is My?

▲ Halloween celebrations and ideas are often found in magazines.

▲ Cut out pictures of various Halloween symbols, such as cats, apples, pumpkins, etc.

▲ Put three pictures on the floor in front of you and your toddler.

▲ Ask a question, such as, "Where is a cat?"

▲ Pick up the cat picture and say, "Oh, here it is."

▲ Ask another question, such as, "Where is a pumpkin?" Pick up the pumpkin picture and say, "Oh, here it is."

▲ Now ask the first question again. "Where is a cat?" Encourage your child to pick it up as you say, "Oh, there it is."

▲ When your toddler can play this game easily, add more objects to the game.

What your toddler will learn

▼

Observation skills

▲ seasonal games

Grasshoppers

▲ In the summer time you can usually find grasshoppers outside.

▲ Show your toddler pictures of grasshoppers.

▲ Go outside and look for grasshoppers.

▲ It's great fun to watch grasshoppers hop. Try to imitate the way they hop.

▲ Pretend to be grasshoppers. Hop around with your toddler.

▲ Try to make a noise like a grasshopper.

What your toddler will learn
▼
Coordination

What Shall We Do?

▲▼▲▼▲▼▲▼▲▼▲▼▲▼▲▼▲▼▲▼▲▼▲▼▲▼▲▼

▲ This is a good game to play outside in the spring or in the summer.

▲ Walk around the yard with your toddler and talk about the different things that you see. The trees, the grass, rocks, flowers are just a few things that will probably be in your immediate view.

▲ After you have talked about things in the yard, use the same words in the following game.

> *One, two*
>
> *Me and you*
>
> *What shall we do today?*
>
> *Let's touch the grass (touch the grass)*
>
> *I love the grass, don't you?*

▲ Repeat the poem and touch something else that you have talked about.

▲ To make the game just a little harder, try touching two things.

What your toddler will learn

▼

Language skills

▲ seasonal games

The Butterfly Game

▲ Show your toddler pictures of a butterfly. Talk about the beautiful colors and the wings.

▲ Show your toddler how to make his arms become butterfly wings. Fly around the room.

▲ Play a butterfly game. The following rhyme tells the butterfly to fly to a different object. Make up the objects that are in your own environment.

> *Butterfly, butterfly*
>
> *Flutter by, flutter by*
>
> *Butterfly, butterfly*
>
> *Fly to the door. (fly to the door and touch it)*

▲ Repeat the poem and change the last line each time.

▲ Now ask your child to tell you where the butterfly should go.

What your toddler will learn
▼
Listening skills

seasonal games ▲

Spring Movements

▲▼▲▼▲▼▲▼▲▼▲▼▲▼▲▼▲▼▲▼▲▼▲▼▲▼▲

▲ Play this game outside on a lovely spring day.

▲ Pick two or three movements that you can do with your child, for example, walking, running and jumping.

▲ Tell your toddler that you are going to walk to the tree. Holding your child's hand, walk to a tree and stop.

▲ Next tell your toddler that you are going to run to the door. Holding your child's hand, run to the door.

▲ Continue running, walking or jumping to a designated spot.

What your toddler will learn

▼

Coordination

▲▼▲▼▲▼▲▼▲▼▲▼▲▼▲▼▲▼▲▼▲▼▲▼▲▼▲

▲ seasonal games

Snow Pictures

▲▼▲▼▲▼▲▼▲▼▲▼▲▼▲▼▲▼▲▼▲▼▲▼▲▼▲▼▲

▲ This game should be played when you can see snow on the ground.

▲ Give your toddler white paper and let him tear it into small pieces.

▲ Take a piece of blue construction paper and place it on a table.

▲ Put some glue on a piece of the paper and let your toddler place the "snowflakes" on the blue paper.

▲ When the picture is finished, hang it on the wall for all to see.

What your toddler will learn
▼
Creativity

▲▼▲▼▲▼▲▼▲▼▲▼▲▼▲▼▲▼▲▼▲▼▲▼▲▼▲▼▲

seasonal games ▲

Sticky Fun

▲▼▲▼▲▼▲▼▲▼▲▼▲▼▲▼▲▼▲▼▲▼▲▼▲▼▲

▲ This game takes a little work on the part of the adult, but you will find that it is worth it when you see the joy your toddler will experience.

▲ Make a sticky board by putting clear self-adhesive paper over heavy cardboard. The cardboard should be about the size of a place mat.

▲ Take the backing off of the paper so that the sticky part is facing up.

▲ Then take adhesive paper and frame the sticky part along all four sides.

▲ Have precut pictures from magazines that your child can pick up and stick on to the paper.

▲ A fall theme of pictures might be trees, squirrels, apples, etc. Select pictures appropriate to the season.

▲ This is a game your toddler will want to play many, many times.

What your toddler will learn

▼

Fine motor skills

▲▼▲▼▲▼▲▼▲▼▲▼▲▼▲▼▲▼▲▼▲▼▲▼▲▼▲

I Hear Thunder

▲▽▲▽▲▽▲▽▲▽▲▽▲▽▲▽▲▽▲▽▲▽▲▽▲▽▲▽▲

▲ Children are fascinated with thunder. Sometimes they are frightened and a song can calm them down.

▲ Sing this song to the tune of "Frere Jacques."

> *I hear thunder, I hear thunder. (stamp your feet on the floor to make the thunder)*
>
> *Listen now, listen now. (put your hand to your ear)*
>
> *Pitter patter raindrops,*
>
> *Pitter patter raindrops, (wiggle your fingers in the air)*
>
> *Now it's through, now it's through.*

What your toddler will learn

▼

Listening skills

▲▽▲▽▲▽▲▽▲▽▲▽▲▽▲▽▲▽▲▽▲▽▲▽▲▽▲▽▲

Footprints in the Snow

▲▼▲▼▲▼▲▼▲▼▲▼▲▼▲▼▲▼▲▼▲▼▲▼▲▼▲▼▲

▲ When the ground is covered with snow, it is fascinating to walk outside and study footprints.

▲ Take your toddler outside and look for prints in the snow. Try to figure out what bird or animal made those footprints.

▲ Let your toddler put his hand in the snow and look at his handprint.

▲ Put your hand in the snow and compare your print with your toddler's print.

▲ Compare your shoe or boot prints to your toddlers.

▲ This is a game that I still like to play.

What your toddler will learn
▼
Observation skills

▲ seasonal games

Singing Games

▲▽▲▽▲▽▲▽▲▽▲▽▲▽▲▽▲▽▲▽▲▽▲▽▲▽▲▽▲▽▲▽▲

▲▽▲▽▲▽▲▽▲▽▲▽▲▽▲▽▲▽▲▽▲▽▲▽▲▽▲▽▲▽▲▽▲

Looby Loo

▲ "Looby Loo" is a popular singing game and wonderful for teaching your toddler about parts of the body.

▲ Sit your toddler on your lap facing you and sing the song.

▲ As you sing about the different parts of the body, move the appropriate part of your child's body.

> *Here we go looby loo, (bounce your knees)*
>
> *Here we go looby lie, (keep bouncing)*
>
> *Here we go looby loo,*
>
> *All on a Saturday night.*

> *You put your right hand in, (move your child's hand)*
>
> *You put your right hand out, (move your child's hand)*
>
> *You give your hand a shake, shake, shake, (shake your child's hand)*
>
> *And move yourself about. (start bouncing again)*

▲ Sing again about the left hand, right foot, left foot and head.

What your toddler will learn
▼
About parts of the body

Spin Around

▲▼▲▼▲▼▲▼▲▼▲▼▲▼▲▼▲▼▲▼▲▼▲▼▲▼▲

▲ Spinning around with your toddler is always great fun, especially if you are holding her in your arms as you spin.

▲ Spin for short periods of time so that neither of you will get dizzy.

▲ Hold your child in your arms in a rocking motion or upright with her head over one of your shoulders.

▲ Sing as you spin. Any song that you choose will be just fine.

What your toddler will learn
▼
Balance

▲▼▲▼▲▼▲▼▲▼▲▼▲▼▲▼▲▼▲▼▲▼▲▼▲▼▲

My Bonnie

▲ Hold your toddler in your arms and rock him back and forth as you sing the song "My Bonnie Lies Over the Ocean."

My Bonnie lies over the ocean.

My Bonnie lies over the sea.

My Bonnie lies over the ocean.

Oh, bring back my Bonnie to me.

▲ As you rock your child back and forth, make your arms swoop up and down bigger and bigger.

▲ In the next part of the song, move your child forward and back.

Bring back, bring back

Oh, bring back my Bonnie to me, to me.

Bring back, bring back

Oh, bring back my Bonnie to me.

▲ Change the word "Bonnie" to the name of your child.

What your toddler will learn

▼

Bonding

singing games ▲

Rock-a-bye Baby

▲▽▲▽▲▽▲▽▲▽▲▽▲▽▲▽▲▽▲▽▲▽▲▽▲▽▲▽▲▽▲

▲ Hold your child in your arms and rock him back and forth as you sing "Rock-a-bye Baby."

▲ A rocking motion is both calming and enjoyable.

> *Rock-a-bye baby*
>
> *On the tree top.*
>
> *When the wind blows*
>
> *The cradle will rock.*
>
> *When the bough breaks*
>
> *The cradle will fall,*
>
> *And down will come baby*
>
> *Cradle and all.*

▲ On the last two lines hold your toddler close and give him a big hug.

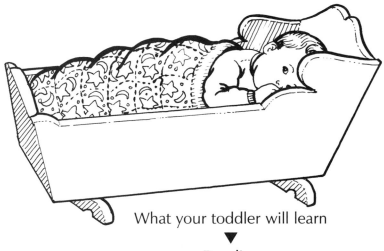

What your toddler will learn

▼

Bonding

▲▽▲▽▲▽▲▽▲▽▲▽▲▽▲▽▲▽▲▽▲▽▲▽▲▽▲▽▲▽▲

▲ singing games

Little Boy (or Girl)

▲▼▲▼▲▼▲▼▲▼▲▼▲▼▲▼▲▼▲▼▲▼▲▼▲▼▲▼▲▼▲

▲ This game is sung to the tune of "London Bridge."

▲ Sit on the floor with your toddler and sing the following song.

> *Little boy will you come here,*
>
> *You come here, you come here?*
>
> *Little boy will you come here,*
>
> *And help me with my jumping?*

▲ Jump up and down. If your child can stand, help him hop up and down. If not, hold him in your arms and hop.

▲ Continue singing the song and change the motor skill each time.

▲ Ideas include:

> *...help me with my marching?*
>
> *...help me with my swimming?*
>
> *...help me with my dancing?*
>
> *...help me with my clapping?*

What your toddler will learn
▼
Coordination

▲▼▲▼▲▼▲▼▲▼▲▼▲▼▲▼▲▼▲▼▲▼▲▼▲▼▲▼▲▼▲

This a Way, That a Way

▲▼▲▼▲▼▲▼▲▼▲▼▲▼▲▼▲▼▲▼▲▼▲▼▲▼▲

▲ The words of this song are adapted from a song by Huddie Ledbetter popularly known as Leadbelly.

▲ Hold your toddler in your arms and dance around the room as you sing this wonderful old folk song. If you don't know the melody, say the words in a rhythmic pattern.

> *Ha, ha, this a way*
> *Ha, ha, that a way*
> *Ha, ha, this a way*
> *Then, tho, then.*

> *When I was a little girl, little girl, little girl*
> *When I was a little girl*
> *Then, tho, then.*

▲ Sing about things that your toddler can do. For example:

> *I played with my daddy, daddy, daddy,*
> *I played with my daddy*
> *Then, tho, then.*

▲ Additional suggestions include:

> *I went to the supermarket...*
> *I played with my toys...*
> *I liked taking a bath...*

What your toddler will learn

▼

Rhythm

▲▼▲▼▲▼▲▼▲▼▲▼▲▼▲▼▲▼▲▼▲▼▲▼▲▼▲

▲ singing games

Make a noise

▲▼▲▼▲▼▲▼▲▼▲▼▲▼▲▼▲▼▲▼▲▼▲▼▲▼▲

▲ Play the following game with your toddler. Show her how to clap loudly and softly.

>*Let your hands (clap, clap)*
>
>*Make a noise (clap, clap)*
>
>*Make it soft (clap, clap)*
>
>*Make it low (clap, clap)*
>
>*Let your hands (clap, clap)*
>
>*Make a noise (clap, clap)*
>
>*Let it grow and grow and grow (keep clapping louder each time)*
>
>*Until the air all around is full of sound.*

▲ Make up more verses using your feet, your mouth, etc.

What your toddler will learn
▼
About loud and soft

▲▼▲▼▲▼▲▼▲▼▲▼▲▼▲▼▲▼▲▼▲▼▲▼▲▼▲

singing games ▲

Rattles and Shakers

▲▼▲▼▲▼▲▼▲▼▲▼▲▼▲▼▲▼▲▼▲▼▲▼▲▼▲▼

▲ You can make a rattle or a shaker from a plastic container or a plastic egg cup.

▲ The container needs to have a lid that is securely fastened.

▲ Put a variety of things in the container such as dried peas or beans, rice, tapioca, buttons, marbles, washers, etc. Different items create different sounds. Experiment with different materials.

▲ It is also interesting to change the amount in each container. The sound will change.

▲ Decorate your shaker and let your toddler hold it and shake it.

▲ It's important to supervise this activity just in case the shaker should open.

▲ Take your shakers, march around the room and sing your favorite songs.

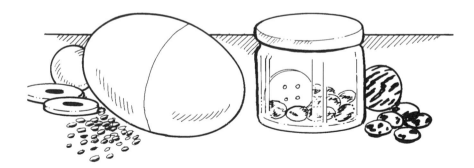

What your toddler will learn
▼
About sounds

▲▼▲▼▲▼▲▼▲▼▲▼▲▼▲▼▲▼▲▼▲▼▲▼▲▼▲▼

▲ singing games

One Button

▲▼▲▼▲▼▲▼▲▼▲▼▲▼▲▼▲▼▲▼▲▼▲▼▲▼▲▼▲▼▲

▲ When buttoning your toddler's coat or sweater, sing up the scale.

▲ When unbuttoning, sing down the scale.

One button (do)

Two buttons (re)

Three buttons (mi)

Four (fa)

Five buttons (so)

Six buttons (la)

Seven buttons (ti)

More (do)

What your toddler will learn

▼

About the scale

▲▼▲▼▲▼▲▼▲▼▲▼▲▼▲▼▲▼▲▼▲▼▲▼▲▼▲▼▲▼▲

The Happy Game

▲▼▲▼▲▼▲▼▲▼▲▼▲▼▲▼▲▼▲▼▲▼▲▼▲▼▲▼▲▼▲▼▲

▲ Sit on the floor with your toddler facing you.

▲ Sing the song "If You're Happy and You Know It."

> *If you're happy and you know it, clap your hands. (take your toddler's hands and clap them together)*
>
> *If you're happy and you know it, clap your hands. (repeat clapping)*
>
> *If you're happy and you know it,*
>
> *Then your smile will surely show it.*
>
> *If you're happy and you know it, clap your hands. (repeat clapping)*

▲ Keep repeating the song and change the action.

▲ Move your toddler's hands for clapping, waving, etc. Do the action first and then let your toddler do it.

What your toddler will learn
▼
Coordination

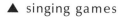

▲ singing games

A Hunting We Will Go

▲▼▲▼▲▼▲▼▲▼▲▼▲▼▲▼▲▼▲▼▲▼▲▼▲▼▲▼▲▼▲

▲ Sing the song "A Hunting We Will Go."

▲ As you are singing the song, pretend to hide from your toddler.

▲ On the words "catch a fox" run out and catch her in your arms.

▲ Once she knows how to play the game, switch parts and let her hide from you.

> *A hunting we will go.*
>
> *A hunting we will go.*
>
> *We'll catch a fox and put it in a box,*
>
> *And never let it go.*

▲ You can change the word "fox" to the name of your child.

What your toddler will learn

▼

Fun

▲▼▲▼▲▼▲▼▲▼▲▼▲▼▲▼▲▼▲▼▲▼▲▼▲▼▲▼▲▼▲

Comin' 'Round the Mountain

▲▼▲▼▲▼▲▼▲▼▲▼▲▼▲▼▲▼▲▼▲▼▲▼▲▼▲▼▲

▲ Hold your toddler in your arms as you sing this familiar folk song. As you sing each verse, do the actions.

She'll be comin' 'round the mountain when she comes.

She'll be comin' 'round the mountain when she comes.

She'll be comin' 'round the mountain,

She'll be comin' 'round the mountain,

She'll be comin' 'round the mountain when she comes. (dance around the room)

She'll be drivin' six white horses... (pretend to drive)

And we'll all go out to meet her... (wave "hi")

And we'll all eat chicken and dumplings... (rub your tummy)

What your toddler will learn

▼

Language skills

▲ singing games

212

Where Is Lucy?

▲▼▲▼▲▼▲▼▲▼▲▼▲▼▲▼▲▼▲▼▲▼▲▼▲▼▲

▲ Sing to the tune of "Frere Jacques."

> *Where is Lucy? (fill in child's name)*
>
> *Where is Lucy?*
>
> *Here I am, here I am. (hold your child's arms high over her head)*
>
> *Clap your little hands,*
>
> *Clap your little hands, (clap your child's hands together)*
>
> *Hip, hip, hooray!*
>
> *Hip, hip, hooray!*

▲ Repeat the song and change the action. Instead of "Clap your little hands," you could say, "Touch your little nose" or "Wave your little hands."

▲ Think of the kinds of actions that your child can do and incorporate them in the song.

What your toddler will learn
▼
Language skills

▲▼▲▼▲▼▲▼▲▼▲▼▲▼▲▼▲▼▲▼▲▼▲▼▲▼▲

Clap Your Hands

▲▼▲▼▲▼▲▼▲▼▲▼▲▼▲▼▲▼▲▼▲▼▲▼▲▼▲▼▲▼▲

▲ Sing the following to the tune of "Row, Row, Row Your Boat."

▲ Sing the first verse slowly.

▲ Sing the second verse faster.

> *Clap, clap, clap your hands*
>
> *Slowly every day. (clap your hands slowly)*
>
> *Merrily, merrily, merrily, merrily (keep clapping)*
>
> *Then we shout "Hooray." (shout "hooray")*
>
> *Clap, clap, clap your hands*
>
> *Faster every day. (clap your hands faster)*
>
> *Merrily, merrily, merrily, merrily*
>
> *Then we shout "Hooray." (shout "hooray")*
>
> *Jackie Silberg*

▲ Sing this song with different actions. Always start slowly and go faster. When children are participating in a fast and slow activity, they begin to internalize the concepts.

▲ Other ideas are:

> *roll your hands*   *shake your hands*
>
> *wave your hands*   *stamp your feet*
>
> *shake your hips*

What your toddler will learn
▼
About fast and slow

▲▼▲▼▲▼▲▼▲▼▲▼▲▼▲▼▲▼▲▼▲▼▲▼▲▼▲▼▲▼▲

▲ singing games

Who's That Tapping?

▲▼▲▼▲▼▲▼▲▼▲▼▲▼▲▼▲▼▲▼▲▼▲▼▲▼▲

▲ Show your toddler how to tap her hands lightly on a table top.

▲ Now, show your toddler how to make a fist and knock loudly on the table.

▲ Practice tapping and knocking.

▲ Sing this song to the tune of "Skip To My Lou."

> *Who's that tapping at the window? (tap on the table)*
>
> *Who's that knocking at the door? (knock on the table)*
>
> *(Child's name)'s tapping at the window.*
>
> *I am knocking at the door.*

▲ Use names of family members, friends and animals.

What your toddler will learn

▼

About loud and soft

▲▼▲▼▲▼▲▼▲▼▲▼▲▼▲▼▲▼▲▼▲▼▲▼▲▼▲

singing games ▲

Rhythm Fun

▲ Sit on the floor next to your toddler and give him and yourself a rhythm stick (or a wooden spoon).

▲ Show your child how to hit the stick on the floor gently.

▲ Experiment with your child. Hit the stick loudly and say the word "loud" as you do it. Then try hitting softly and saying the word "soft" as you do it.

▲ Do the same thing hitting the stick fast and then slowly.

▲ Once your toddler understands the words and can control the stick, give him directions and see if he can do what you say.

> *Hit your stick fast.*
>
> *Hit your stick slowly.*
>
> *Hit your stick loud.*
>
> *Hit your stick softly.*

▲ Experiment with hitting the stick on different surfaces, for example, on a carpet and on a floor.

What your toddler will learn
▼
About loud and soft

Let's Play Train

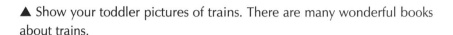

▲ Show your toddler pictures of trains. There are many wonderful books about trains.

▲ Make the sounds that a train makes.

> *Choo choo*
>
> *Chug chug*
>
> *Woo Woo*
>
> *All aboard*

▲ Take four or five chairs and line them up one behind the other.

▲ Tell your child that he is the engineer and sit him on the first chair.

▲ Sing songs about trains such as "Down By the Station" and "Little Red Caboose."

▲ Add the train sounds that you have been practicing to the songs.

What your toddler will learn
▼
About trains

singing games ▲

Clapping Games

▲▼▲▼▲▼▲▼▲▼▲▼▲▼▲▼▲▼▲▼▲▼▲▼▲▼▲▼▲▼▲

▲ There are many ways to clap with your child. Pick a song that is fun to sing like "This Old Man" and experiment with all the different ways that you can clap.

▲ Put your toddler in your lap with her palms down on your palms. As you sing the song, clap your hands upward to hers.

▲ Put your hands in front of your toddler and clap them together.

▲ Take your toddler's hands and let them clap on yours.

▲ Take your toddler's hands and clap them together.

What your toddler will learn
▼
Coordination

▲▼▲▼▲▼▲▼▲▼▲▼▲▼▲▼▲▼▲▼▲▼▲▼▲▼▲▼▲▼▲

▲ singing games

Wiggle Waggle

▲▼▲▼▲▼▲▼▲▼▲▼▲▼▲▼▲▼▲▼▲▼▲▼▲▼▲▼

▲ Hold your hands in front of you and show your toddler how to wiggle his fingers.

▲ Sing this song to the tune of "London Bridge."

Fingers like to wiggle, waggle

Wiggle, waggle, wiggle, waggle. (wiggle your fingers)

Fingers like to wiggle, waggle

On your head. (put your fingers on your head)

▲ Keep singing the song and "wiggle, waggle" your fingers in different places, on your knee, on your toe, behind you and in front of you.

What your toddler will learn
▼
Fine motor skills

Hello, Door

▲▼▲▼▲▼▲▼▲▼▲▼▲▼▲▼▲▼▲▼▲▼▲▼▲▼▲▼

▲ Hold your little one in your arms, dance around the room and sing the following. Make up any tune.

Dancing, dancing, we are dancing.

Dancing, dancing to the door.

▲ Dance to the door. Let your child touch the door. Say, "hello, door."

▲ Sing the song again.

Dancing, dancing, we are dancing.

Dancing, dancing to the chair.

▲ Dance to the chair. Encourage your child to touch the chair. Say, "Hello, chair."

▲ Continue, naming other things in the house.

What your toddler will learn

▼

Fun

▲▼▲▼▲▼▲▼▲▼▲▼▲▼▲▼▲▼▲▼▲▼▲▼▲▼▲▼

▲ singing games

Sing With a Friend

▲▼▲▼▲▼▲▼▲▼▲▼▲▼▲▼▲▼▲▼▲▼▲▼▲▼▲

▲ Dolls and stuffed animals are very special friends to toddlers.

▲ Singing with a stuffed animal will help develop your child's language skills.

▲ Take a stuffed animal and put it in your lap.

▲ Sing the song "Pop Goes the Weasel." On the word "pop" take the stuffed animal and hold it high in the air.

▲ Give the stuffed animal to your toddler and help him hold it high in the air on the word "pop."

▲ Here are the words to "Pop Goes the Weasel."

> *All around the cobbler's bench,*
>
> *The monkey chased the weasel.*
>
> *The monkey laughed to see such fun.*
>
> *Pop! goes the weasel.*

What your toddler will learn
▼
Language skills

▲▼▲▼▲▼▲▼▲▼▲▼▲▼▲▼▲▼▲▼▲▼▲▼▲▼▲

The Radio Game

▲▼▲▼▲▼▲▼▲▼▲▼▲▼▲▼▲▼▲▼▲▼▲▼▲▼▲▼▲▼▲

▲ What does a toddler love to do? You're right. Turn dials and push buttons.

▲ Turning a radio dial can be a source of fun and enjoyment. It also helps develop your child's listening skills.

▲ Show your child how to turn the dial to get different kinds of music.

▲ Play a game. Your toddler turns the dial or pushes the button until you say "Stop."

▲ When you stop, dance according to the kind of music that is playing.

What your toddler will learn
▼
Listening skills

▲▼▲▼▲▼▲▼▲▼▲▼▲▼▲▼▲▼▲▼▲▼▲▼▲▼▲▼▲▼▲

▲ singing games

A Tisket, a Tasket

▲▼▲▼▲▼▲▼▲▼▲▼▲▼▲▼▲▼▲▼▲▼▲▼▲▼▲

▲ You will need a small basket and an envelope to put inside the basket.

▲ Hold your toddler's hand as you walk around the room and sing the song "A Tisket, a Tasket."

▲ When you come to the words "I dropped it" put the basket down.

▲ When the song is finished, ask your toddler to find the basket.

> *A tisket, a tasket*
>
> *A very pretty basket.*
>
> *I wrote a letter to my mom,*
>
> *And on the way I lost it.*

▲ Ask your toddler, "Can you find the basket?"

▲ When he finds the basket, take out the envelope and pretend to read it.

What your toddler will learn

▼

Observation skills

▲▼▲▼▲▼▲▼▲▼▲▼▲▼▲▼▲▼▲▼▲▼▲▼▲▼▲

singing games ▲

A Different Twinkle

▲▼▲▼▲▼▲▼▲▼▲▼▲▼▲▼▲▼▲▼▲▼▲▼▲▼▲

▲ Hold your child in your arms and dance around the room as you sing "Twinkle, Twinkle, Little Star."

▲ At the end of each line stop briefly. This will give your child a physical feeling of the rhythm and the phrasing of the song.

Twinkle, twinkle, little star,

How I wonder what you are.

Up above the earth so high,

Like a diamond in the sky.

Twinkle, twinkle, little star,

How I wonder what you are.

What your toddler will learn

▼

Rhythm

▲▼▲▼▲▼▲▼▲▼▲▼▲▼▲▼▲▼▲▼▲▼▲▼▲▼▲

▲ singing games

The Music Store

▲▼▲▼▲▼▲▼▲▼▲▼▲▼▲▼▲▼▲▼▲▼▲▼▲▼▲▼▲

▲ Take your toddler to a music store.

▲ If you have a friendly salesperson, she might let your child play on the piano.

▲ Show her the drums and try to get someone to demonstrate.

▲ Walk around the store pointing out all of the instruments.

▲ Go home and play music that uses a piano or a drum. Name the instruments of the music as you listen.

What your toddler will learn
▼
About instruments

▲▼▲▼▲▼▲▼▲▼▲▼▲▼▲▼▲▼▲▼▲▼▲▼▲▼▲▼▲

singing games ▲

Music

▲▼▲▼▲▼▲▼▲▼▲▼▲▼▲▼▲▼▲▼▲▼▲▼▲▼▲

▲ Say the following poem and act out the feeling after each line. For example, say the words, "Music can be funny" and then laugh out loud.

> *Music can be funny. (laugh)*
>
> *Music can be sad. (cry)*
>
> *Music makes you happy. (ha, ha, ha)*
>
> *Music makes you mad. (grrrrr)*
>
> *Music can go up. (make your voice go up as you say this line)*
>
> *Music can go down. (make your voice go down as you say this line)*
>
> *Music can be fast or slow. (say fast quickly and slow slowly)*
>
> *Music can be loud or soft. (say loud loudly and soft softly)*

What your toddler will learn

▼

About music

▲ singing games

Marching

▲ Get out some pots and pans that you don't mind having banged around.

▲ Play march music and show your child how to bang the lids together to the music.

▲ As you march around the room, encourage your toddler to lift his legs up high for marching.

▲ You can also take a spoon and hit it on the pot or lid for marching sounds.

▲ Play a game of stopping and starting. Each time you stop the music, the marching and banging stops too.

What your toddler will learn
▼
Coordination

singing games ▲

Ring a Ring of Roses

▲▼▲▼▲▼▲▼▲▼▲▼▲▼▲▼▲▼▲▼▲▼▲▼▲▼▲▼▲

▲ "Ring a Ring of Roses" is a favorite game of toddlers. There are many different words to this familiar game. Here are some others that you might like to try.

▲ Always play the game in the same way by falling down on the last line.

> *A ring a ring o' roses,*
>
> *A pocket full of posies.*
>
> *A-tishoo, a-tishoo,*
>
> *We all fall down.*

> *Ring a ring o' roses,*
>
> *A pocket full of posies.*
>
> *One for Jack and one for Jim,*
>
> *And one for little Moses. (make up your own names for this one)*

> *Ring a ring a row-o*
>
> *See the children go-o*
>
> *Sit below the berry bush*
>
> *They all cry, "Hush, hush, hush."*

What your toddler will learn

▼

Fun

▲▼▲▼▲▼▲▼▲▼▲▼▲▼▲▼▲▼▲▼▲▼▲▼▲▼▲▼▲

Social Games

▲▽▲▽▲▽▲▽▲▽▲▽▲▽▲▽▲▽▲▽▲▽▲▽▲▽▲▽▲▽▲▽▲

▲▽▲▽▲▽▲▽▲▽▲▽▲▽▲▽▲▽▲▽▲▽▲▽▲▽▲▽▲▽▲▽▲

Washing and Drying

▲▼▲▼▲▼▲▼▲▼▲▼▲▼▲▼▲▼▲▼▲▼▲▼▲▼▲▼▲

▲ Washing and drying hands is a motor skill that needs to be taught to a young child.

▲ Singing a song as you wash and dry your hands make this job much more fun.

▲ Sing to the tune of "Eensy Weensy Spider."

Wash your little fingers

Wash them nice and clean

Wash your little fingers

Wash them nice and clean

Dry your little fingers

Get them nice and dry

And, dry your little fingers

Get them nice and dry.

What your toddler will learn
▼
About washing hands

▲▼▲▼▲▼▲▼▲▼▲▼▲▼▲▼▲▼▲▼▲▼▲▼▲▼▲▼▲

social games ▲

At the Castle Gate

▲▼▲▼▲▼▲▼▲▼▲▼▲▼▲▼▲▼▲▼▲▼▲▼▲▼▲▼▲

▲ Sit your toddler in your lap.

▲ Take her hand in yours and show her how to close her fingers and make a fist.

▲ Say the following rhyme as you gently knock your child's fist with your fist.

> Sara's at the castle gate. *(use your toddler's name)*
>
> Sara's at the castle gate.
>
> Sara's at the castle gate.
>
> Open the door and let her in. *(show your toddler how to open her fist)*

▲ When the fist is open, take your fingers and tickle the palm of her hand.

What your toddler will learn
▼
Bonding

▲▼▲▼▲▼▲▼▲▼▲▼▲▼▲▼▲▼▲▼▲▼▲▼▲▼▲▼▲

▲ social games

Mine and Yours

▲▽▲▽▲▽▲▽▲▽▲▽▲▽▲▽▲▽▲▽▲▽▲▽▲▽▲▽▲

▲ It's been said that a toddler's philosophy of life is "What's mine is mine, what's yours is mine, what's his is mine."

▲ Learning the difference between mine and yours will come more easily if you help your child know which objects are definitely his and which objects are yours.

▲ Gather together objects that belong to you—your purse, your comb, your glasses. Mix them up with several of your child's belongings.

▲ Say to your child, "Will you give me my glasses?" When he gives them to you, say, "Thank you, these are my glasses. They are mine."

▲ Now give your child one of his toys and say, "This is your doll. It is yours."

▲ Continue with the rest of the objects.

▲ This game is a gentle way of teaching mine and yours.

What your toddler will learn
▼
About mine and yours

▲▽▲▽▲▽▲▽▲▽▲▽▲▽▲▽▲▽▲▽▲▽▲▽▲▽▲▽▲

social games ▲

Spoon Feeding

▲▼▲▼▲▼▲▼▲▼▲▼▲▼▲▼▲▼▲▼▲▼▲▼▲▼▲▼

▲ Eating with a spoon is an important social skill for your toddler.

▲ Before you attempt to teach your child how to use a spoon, give him spoons to play with.

▲ He will bang them, drop them and probably put them in his mouth.

▲ When you think he is ready to play this game, put a small piece of banana on a spoon and put it in your mouth.

▲ Put a small piece of banana on a spoon and put it in your child's mouth.

▲ Put a spoon in your toddler's hand with a small piece of banana in it. Guide the spoon to your child's mouth.

▲ Keep playing this game with different kinds of food and soon he will be putting the spoon in a bowl of food and feeding himself.

What your toddler will learn
▼
About using a spoon

▲▼▲▼▲▼▲▼▲▼▲▼▲▼▲▼▲▼▲▼▲▼▲▼▲▼▲▼

▲ social games

Wind the Bobbin

▲▼▲▼▲▼▲▼▲▼▲▼▲▼▲▼▲▼▲▼▲▼▲▼▲▼▲▼▲

▲ This is a good game for diaper changes.

▲ Take your toddler's hands and roll them over each other. As you do this, say the following rhyme.

> *Wind the bobbin up*
>
> *Wind the bobbin up*
>
> *Pull, pull (take her hands and pull them apart)*
>
> *Tug, tug, tug. (take her hands and put them back)*

▲ Try the same game using your child's feet.

What your toddler will learn

▼

Cooperation

▲▼▲▼▲▼▲▼▲▼▲▼▲▼▲▼▲▼▲▼▲▼▲▼▲▼▲▼▲

social games ▲

Hot Cross Buns

▲▼▲▼▲▼▲▼▲▼▲▼▲▼▲▼▲▼▲▼▲▼▲▼▲▼▲▼▲▼▲

▲ Say the poem "Hot Cross Buns" with your child.

▲ Sit on the floor facing your toddler. Put her hands in yours. As you say the poem, alternate hitting your thighs and your hands together.

> *Hot cross buns, hot cross buns*
>
> *One a penny, two a penny*
>
> *Hot cross buns.*
>
> *If you have no daughters, give them to your sons*
>
> *Hot cross buns, hot cross buns.*

▲ The history of hot cross buns is fascinating. There are lots of superstitions about them. It was once believed that the buns baked early on Good Friday would have special powers.

▲ Sailors thought that if they took a hot cross bun to sea, it would safeguard them from shipwrecks.

▲ It is thought that the rhyme "Hot Cross Buns" was an advertising cry from the time when bakers sold their wares in the street.

What your toddler will learn
▼
Coordination

▲▼▲▼▲▼▲▼▲▼▲▼▲▼▲▼▲▼▲▼▲▼▲▼▲▼▲▼▲▼▲

Wiggle Your Eyebrows

▲▼▲▼▲▼▲▼▲▼▲▼▲▼▲▼▲▼▲▼▲▼▲▼▲▼▲▼▲

▲ Look in the mirror with your toddler. Point out her eyebrows.

▲ Let her touch your eyebrows. Show her how to wiggle her eyebrows.

▲ Sing the following song to the tune of "Skip To My Lou."

> *Clap your hands and stamp your feet*
>
> *Clap your hands and stamp your feet*
>
> *Clap your hands and stamp your feet*
>
> *Wiggle your eyebrows now.*
>
> *Touch your toes and touch your nose*
>
> *Touch your toes and touch your nose*
>
> *Touch your toes and touch your nose*
>
> *Wiggle your eyebrows now.*

▲ Make up your own verses.

What your toddler will learn
▼
Imitation skills

▲▼▲▼▲▼▲▼▲▼▲▼▲▼▲▼▲▼▲▼▲▼▲▼▲▼▲▼▲

social games ▲

Telephone Talk

▲▼▲▼▲▼▲▼▲▼▲▼▲▼▲▼▲▼▲▼▲▼▲▼▲▼▲▼▲

▲ As you know, toddlers love the phone. They like to imitate you talking as well as play and chew on the telephone cord.

▲ Take a phone and let your toddler listen to the dial tone.

▲ Dial a member of your family or a friend and let her listen to their voice on the phone.

▲ Encourage your child to say "Bye-bye" to the voice.

▲ Call numbers that have an automatic message and let your toddler listen to the message.

▲ When calling an automatic message, ask a question first about the message. For example, "I wonder what time it is. Let's call the time and find out."

▲ You will be amazed at the telephone skills your child will develop.

What your toddler will learn
▼
About the telephone

▲▼▲▼▲▼▲▼▲▼▲▼▲▼▲▼▲▼▲▼▲▼▲▼▲▼▲▼▲

▲ social games

Two in the Boat

▲▼▲▼▲▼▲▼▲▼▲▼▲▼▲▼▲▼▲▼▲▼▲▼▲▼▲▼▲

▲ This game is played with three people.

▲ Two people sit on the floor facing each other and with legs stretched out. Hold hands and rock back and forth.

▲ Put your toddler in the middle.

▲ Rock back and forth as you say:

> *Two in the boat and the waves run high*
>
> *Iwo in the boat and the waves run high*
>
> *Two in the boat and the waves run high*
>
> *Get me a partner by and by.*

▲ Add more people in the boat.

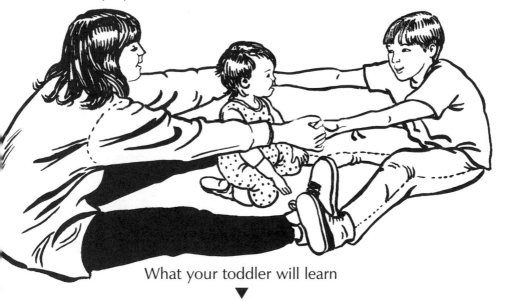

What your toddler will learn
▼
Fun

▲▼▲▼▲▼▲▼▲▼▲▼▲▼▲▼▲▼▲▼▲▼▲▼▲▼▲▼

social games ▲

Fun

▲▼▲▼▲▼▲▼▲▼▲▼▲▼▲▼▲▼▲▼▲▼▲▼▲▼▲▼▲

▲ Eating out with a toddler is wonderful for developing her social skills.

▲ Sometimes toddlers get a little fussy and don't want to cooperate.

▲ Play this game with your child and she will enjoy her restaurant stay.

▲ Take a paper napkin and crunch it into a round ball. Pretend that it is a puppet and talk to your toddler via the puppet.

▲ Take a pen or marker and draw a face on the paper napkin.

▲ Some things you can say are:

> *"Hello, what would you like to eat?"*
>
> *"I love to drink milk, do you?"*
>
> *"What is your name?"*

What your toddler will learn

▼

Imagination

▲▼▲▼▲▼▲▼▲▼▲▼▲▼▲▼▲▼▲▼▲▼▲▼▲▼▲▼▲

▲ social games

Cleaning Up

▲▼▲▼▲▼▲▼▲▼▲▼▲▼▲▼▲▼▲▼▲▼▲▼▲▼▲

▲ Toddlers often protest when you want to wipe their face and hands when they are finished eating.

▲ Take a wet cloth and show your child how you wipe your face and hands.

▲ Give a wet cloth to your child and ask him to wipe his face and hands.

▲ When the meal is finished, give your toddler a sponge or wet cloth to wipe the table.

▲ Toddlers love to please you so give him a lot of praise.

What your toddler will learn
▼
About cleaning up

▲▼▲▼▲▼▲▼▲▼▲▼▲▼▲▼▲▼▲▼▲▼▲▼▲▼▲

social games ▲

Friends

▲▼▲▼▲▼▲▼▲▼▲▼▲▼▲▼▲▼▲▼▲▼▲▼▲▼▲▼▲▼

▲ Invite a friend over to play. This could be an adult or another child.

▲ Take pictures of your toddler with the friend.

▲ After the pictures are developed, talk about them with your child, emphasizing what friends do.

▲ Things to talk about include:

Friends play together

Friends take turns

Friends laugh with you

Friends give you hugs

Friends like to be with you

What your toddler will learn
▼
About friendship

▲▼▲▼▲▼▲▼▲▼▲▼▲▼▲▼▲▼▲▼▲▼▲▼▲▼▲▼▲▼

▲ social games

London Bridge

▲ Two people make a bridge by putting their hands together in front of them like an arch.

▲ Sing the song "London Bridge" and show your toddler how to go under the bridge.

▲ Keep going under the bridge, and when you say, "My fair lady," whoever is under the bridge gets caught.

> *London Bridge is falling down,*
>
> *Falling down, falling down,*
>
> *London Bridge is falling down,*
>
> *My fair lady.*

▲ Whoever is in the middle gets to sway back and forth to the next verse.

> *Build it up with sticks and stones,*
>
> *Sticks and stones, sticks and stones,*
>
> *Build it up with sticks and stones,*
>
> *My fair lady.*

▲ From this point on, make up your verses of what to build it up with, for example, toys and potatoes. Sometimes silly things appeal to a toddler.

What your toddler will learn

▼

Cooperation

social games ▲

My House

▲▼▲▼▲▼▲▼▲▼▲▼▲▼▲▼▲▼▲▼▲▼▲▼▲▼▲▼

▲ Say this fingerplay with your child while you do the actions.

▲ Say it the second time and move your toddler's fingers to form the house.

▲ Say it the third time and let your toddler imitate you.

> *This is my house. (put your fingertips together for the roof)*
>
> *This is the door. (put the tips of your index fingers together*
>
> *The windows are shiny, (pretend you are polishing the windows)*
>
> *And so is the floor. (pretend to polish the floor)*
>
> *Outside there is a chimney, (hold your hands high for the chimney)*
>
> *As tall as can be.*
>
> *With smoke that goes curling up, (wave one hand slowly over your head)*
>
> *Won't you come and see?*

What your toddler will learn
▼
Fine motor skills

▲▼▲▼▲▼▲▼▲▼▲▼▲▼▲▼▲▼▲▼▲▼▲▼▲▼▲▼

▲ social games

Toy Games

▲▼▲▼▲▼▲▼▲▼▲▼▲▼▲▼▲▼▲▼▲▼▲▼▲▼▲▼▲▼▲

▲▼▲▼▲▼▲▼▲▼▲▼▲▼▲▼▲▼▲▼▲▼▲▼▲▼▲▼▲▼▲

Beach Ball Fun

▲▼▲▼▲▼▲▼▲▼▲▼▲▼▲▼▲▼▲▼▲▼▲▼▲▼▲▼▲▼▲

▲ Get a large and colorful beach ball.

▲ Roll the ball to your toddler.

▲ Take a stuffed animal and put it on top of the ball.

▲ Roll the ball back and forth holding the toy.

▲ Ask your child if he would like to sit on the ball.

▲ If your toddler agrees, hold him securely while balancing him on the ball.

▲ As you roll the ball in different directions, say the
corresponding words,
back and forth, side
to side, left and
right.

What your toddler will learn
▼
Balance

▲▼▲▼▲▼▲▼▲▼▲▼▲▼▲▼▲▼▲▼▲▼▲▼▲▼▲▼▲▼▲

toy games ▲

Get the Toy

▲▼▲▼▲▼▲▼▲▼▲▼▲▼▲▼▲▼▲▼▲▼▲▼▲▼▲▼▲

▲ Games that challenge your child's motor skills are fun and exciting for your toddler.

▲ Take a pillow or a cushion and put it in front of a favorite toy.

▲ Show your child where the toy is and then encourage him to get it.

▲ Make the obstacles easy enough so that your child won't be frustrated.

▲ Crawling around and over things develops your child's motor skills and coordination.

▲ To add to the fun, hold your child in your lap and say, "Ready, set, go!" as you let him go to crawl or walk to the toy.

What your toddler will learn
▼
Coordination

▲▼▲▼▲▼▲▼▲▼▲▼▲▼▲▼▲▼▲▼▲▼▲▼▲▼▲▼▲

▲ toy games

Wrapping

▲▼▲▼▲▼▲▼▲▼▲▼▲▼▲▼▲▼▲▼▲▼▲▼▲▼▲

▲ Take two of your child's favorite toys and partially wrap them in tissue paper.

▲ Give the toys to your toddler and encourage him to take off the paper.

▲ When he can do that easily, try other kinds of paper. Wrapping paper, aluminum foil, paper sacks.

▲ Use masking tape on the wrapping so that he can try to remove that too.

▲ Each time your child unwraps the toy, say the name of the toy.

What your toddler will learn
▼
Fine motor skills

▲▼▲▼▲▼▲▼▲▼▲▼▲▼▲▼▲▼▲▼▲▼▲▼▲▼▲

toy games ▲

Peekaboo Box

▲ You will need a box large enough for your toddler to crawl inside.

▲ Cut a hole large enough for your child to put his head through.

▲ Encourage your toddler to crawl into the box.

▲ Play peekaboo with you on the outside and your child on the inside. Either you or your toddler can put your head into the hole and say, "Peekaboo!"

▲ Build anticipation by saying, "One, two, three...peekaboo!"

▲ When you put your head in the hole, change the way you look. Make a funny face, put a scarf on your head or around your neck, put on a pair of glasses. This makes the game even more fun for your child.

What your toddler will learn

▼

Fun

Touch the Toy

▲▼▲▼▲▼▲▼▲▼▲▼▲▼▲▼▲▼▲▼▲▼▲▼▲▼▲▼▲

▲ Put a familiar toy in a box. A shoebox is good to use with this game.

▲ Make a hole in the top of the box large enough for your hand to fit inside.

▲ Have your toddler put her hand in the box and feel the toy.

▲ Now, put your hand in the box and feel the toy.

▲ Repeat this several times so that your toddler has a chance to experience the toy by feel.

▲ Take the toy out of the box and put it on the floor next to another toy.

▲ Your child may be able to identify which toy was in the box because even though she couldn't see the toy in the box, she may recognize it by the way it felt.

What your toddler will learn
▼
Thinking skills

▲▼▲▼▲▼▲▼▲▼▲▼▲▼▲▼▲▼▲▼▲▼▲▼▲▼▲▼▲

toy games ▲

Creep, Creep, Creep

▲▼▲▼▲▼▲▼▲▼▲▼▲▼▲▼▲▼▲▼▲▼▲▼▲▼▲▼▲▼▲

▲ Creep on the floor with your toddler. Show her how to creep very softly.

▲ Place several toys on the floor. Tell your toddler to creep to the toy and wake it up by saying, "Wake up, sleepy head" and clap her hands.

▲ Put some stuffed animals on the floor and show her how to creep up to them and pat them on the head to wake them up. Both of you say, "Wake up, sleepy head" together.

▲ Pretend to be one of the animals. Tell your toddler to creep up to you and wake you up.

▲ This game is lots of fun and your child will want to play it again and again.

What your toddler will learn
▼
About loud and soft

▲▼▲▼▲▼▲▼▲▼▲▼▲▼▲▼▲▼▲▼▲▼▲▼▲▼▲▼▲▼▲

▲ toy games

Pick Up Time

▲▼▲▼▲▼▲▼▲▼▲▼▲▼▲▼▲▼▲▼▲▼▲▼▲▼▲▼

▲ Show your child a container that you want the toys to go in.

▲ Sit with your toddler and put one of her toys into the container.

▲ Now give her a toy and ask her to put it in the container. Praise her for a good job.

▲ Ask your toddler, "What toy would you like to pick up next?"

▲ Keep encouraging her and praising her as she picks up the toy of her choice and puts it in the container.

▲ This is a good time for a song. For example, "This is the way we pick up the toys," sung to the tune of "Mulberry Bush."

What your toddler will learn
▼
Cooperation

▲▼▲▼▲▼▲▼▲▼▲▼▲▼▲▼▲▼▲▼▲▼▲▼▲▼▲▼

toy games ▲

Open the Gates

▲▼▲▼▲▼▲▼▲▼▲▼▲▼▲▼▲▼▲▼▲▼▲▼▲▼▲▼▲

▲ Gather together some of your child's favorite toys.

▲ Show your child how to lie down on his tummy and push his body up in the middle with his hands and legs still on the floor.

▲ When he can do this, play the following game. Each time that you say the words "open the gates," he lifts his body in the middle while keeping his hands and feet on the ground.

> *Open the gates as high as the sky*
>
> *And let the car go passing by. (when your child raises his middle, take a small car or another small toy and move it under him)*
>
> *Jackie Silberg*

▲ The idea is to start with a small toy and keep letting the toy get bigger. Your child will have to raise his tummy higher and higher.

What your toddler will learn
▼
Coordination

▲▼▲▼▲▼▲▼▲▼▲▼▲▼▲▼▲▼▲▼▲▼▲▼▲▼▲▼▲

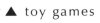

Paper Rain

▲ Toddlers love to tear paper. It makes them feel powerful because they can control what is happening to the paper.

▲ Give your toddler some pages from a used magazine that has interesting pictures on them.

▲ Talk about the pictures and then suggest to your toddler to tear the paper. He may start tearing before you suggest it.

▲ When the paper is torn into pieces, pick them up and put them in a container.

▲ Say to your child, "Here comes the rain." Turn the container over and let the paper rain fall out.

▲ As the rain is falling, sing the song "Rain, rain, go away."

▲ Pick up the paper and start again. Your toddler will love this game and want to play it over and over.

What your toddler will learn
▼
Fine motor skills

toy games ▲

What's in There?

▲▼▲▼▲▼▲▼▲▼▲▼▲▼▲▼▲▼▲▼▲▼▲▼▲▼▲▼

▲ Cardboard toilet paper rolls make great toys for toddlers.

▲ Take a roll and stuff it with a variety of things. Cotton balls, colorful wrapping paper and shiny tinsel are good to try.

▲ In the middle of all of the stuffing, put a small toy.

▲ Show your child how to pull out the stuffing.

▲ As she is taking out the stuffing, ask her questions such as, "What's in there?" or "What are you pulling out?"

▲ When she discovers the toy, shout "Hooray!" and clap your hands.

▲ Soon she will be hiding her own toys and pulling them out.

What your toddler will learn
▼
Fine motor skills

▲▼▲▼▲▼▲▼▲▼▲▼▲▼▲▼▲▼▲▼▲▼▲▼▲▼▲▼

▲ toy games

Pop Up Toy

▲▼▲▼▲▼▲▼▲▼▲▼▲▼▲▼▲▼▲▼▲▼▲▼▲▼▲▼

▲ Make a pop up toy for your toddler. Make a hole in the bottom of a paper cup. Put a straw through the hole.

▲ Attach a round piece of cardboard to one end of the straw. Draw a face on the cardboard.

▲ Show your toddler how to pull the straw and make the face disappear and push up on the straw and make the face appear.

What your toddler will learn
▼
Fine motor skills

▲▼▲▼▲▼▲▼▲▼▲▼▲▼▲▼▲▼▲▼▲▼▲▼▲▼▲▼

toy games ▲

I Love Coffee

▲ Play this game with a stuffed toy.

▲ Put the toy on your toddler's knee and say.

> *I love coffee,*
>
> *I love tea,*
>
> *I love sitting on your knee.*

▲ Now put the toy on your child's head.

> *I love coffee,*
>
> *I love bread,*
>
> *I love sitting on your head.*

▲ Keep playing the game and name different parts of the body. The words do not have to rhyme.

▲ Try playing the game with your toddler. Let him sit on your knee, foot, etc.

What your toddler will learn

▼

Fun

Tubes and More

▲▼▲▼▲▼▲▼▲▼▲▼▲▼▲▼▲▼▲▼▲▼▲▼▲▼▲

▲ Take a paper towel tube and show your child the different things that you can do with it.

▲ Pretend it's a microphone.

▲ Take a small ball and encourage your child to roll it through the tube.

▲ Pretend that it's a baton and lead the band.

▲ Hold it to your eye and pretend it's a telescope.

What your toddler will learn

▼

Imagination

toy games ▲

Purse Toys

▲▼▲▼▲▼▲▼▲▼▲▼▲▼▲▼▲▼▲▼▲▼▲▼▲▼▲▼▲

▲ Some of the best toys can be found right in your own home.

▲ Toddlers love to explore purses.

▲ Fill an empty purse with familiar things, such as, keys, comb, tissue, eyeglasses (best if glass part is missing), money purse.

▲ Ask your child to find an item in the purse. For example, "Would you please give me the car keys?"

▲ When your child finds the keys, praise her for finding them.

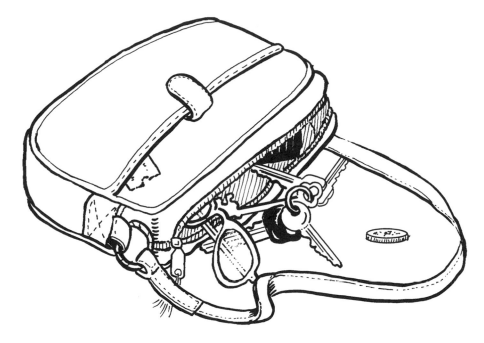

What your toddler will learn
▼
Thinking skills

▲▼▲▼▲▼▲▼▲▼▲▼▲▼▲▼▲▼▲▼▲▼▲▼▲▼▲▼▲

▲ toy games

Where Is the Toy?

▲▼▲▼▲▼▲▼▲▼▲▼▲▼▲▼▲▼▲▼▲▼▲▼▲▼▲▼▲▼

▲ Take two large cups and put them in front of your toddler.

▲ Put one of his favorite toys, such as a ball, under one of the cups.

▲ Ask your child, "Where is the ball?" Lift up the cup that has the ball under it.

▲ Repeat this several times and you will soon find that your child will be lifting the cup before you have a chance.

▲ Add a third cup to make the game a little harder.

What your toddler will learn
▼
Thinking skills

▲▼▲▼▲▼▲▼▲▼▲▼▲▼▲▼▲▼▲▼▲▼▲▼▲▼▲▼▲▼

toy games ▲

Stuffed Fun

▲ Ask your toddler to get her favorite stuffed animal and put it down on the floor next to her.

▲ Sit down on the floor and place a stuffed toy in front of yourself.

▲ Ask your child to do different activities with her stuffed toy.

▲ Ask your child to do something with the stuffed toy. If your toddler doesn't understand, show her by following the direction yourself.

▲ Here are some ideas: pick up your animal's arm, shake its leg, nod its head, move its knee, move its elbow and give it a big hug.

What your toddler will learn
▼
Listening skills

▲ toy games

Take Your Doll

▲ By now your toddler has a favorite stuffed animal or doll. You can use his doll in helping him develop listening skills.

▲ Give your toddler directions for doing different things with his favorite doll.

> *Wiggle (toy's name) toe.*
>
> *Kiss (toy's name) on the head.*
>
> *Shake (toys' name) hand.*

▲ Show your child how to do these activities if he isn't sure how to do them.

▲ Give your toddler ideas of things do with his doll that he does, for example, brush (toy's name) teeth, etc.

What your toddler will learn
▼
Listening skills

toy games ▲

Bowling

▲▼▲▼▲▼▲▼▲▼▲▼▲▼▲▼▲▼▲▼▲▼▲▼▲▼▲▼▲▼▲

▲ Take three or four paper cups and turn them upside down on the floor.

▲ Take a small ball and show your child how to roll the ball and knock down the cups.

▲ Each time that a cup gets knocked down, clap your hands and shout, "Hooray!"

▲ Let your child try knocking down the cups. Have her sit close enough to the cups that she will be successful in knocking them down.

▲ After your toddler has learned to do this well, you can set up groups of cups in several places in the room, and let her try to knock down all of them.

What your toddler will learn

▼

Coordination

▲▼▲▼▲▼▲▼▲▼▲▼▲▼▲▼▲▼▲▼▲▼▲▼▲▼▲▼▲▼▲

Up and Down

▲ Play games with a small xylophone.

▲ Let your toddler experiment with hitting the tones. This takes fine motor skill development to hit the mallet on the tone bar.

▲ Take the mallet and hit each tone from low to high. Sing the scale as you do this.

▲ Now hit the notes and sing the scale downward.

▲ Crouch down with your hands on the floor. Sing the scale again as you move your body upward and stretch your hands high in the sky.

▲ Now come back down as you sing the scale downward.

▲ Don't be surprised to find your child trying to do the same thing in the near future.

What your toddler will learn
▼
Listening skills

toy games ▲

Tape Recorders

▲▼▲▼▲▼▲▼▲▼▲▼▲▼▲▼▲▼▲▼▲▼▲▼▲▼▲▼

▲ Toddlers love to have their own tape players. There are many tape recorders that are very simple to use.

▲ Make up a story using your child's name in the story. Tell the story on tape so that your child can listen to it over and over.

▲ If your child is in child care, listening to a parent's voice is very calming to a young toddler.

▲ Select a variety of tapes for your child. Classical, children's songs, pop tunes and a variety of musical styles.

What your toddler will learn

▼

Listening skills

▲▼▲▼▲▼▲▼▲▼▲▼▲▼▲▼▲▼▲▼▲▼▲▼▲▼▲▼

Books for Toddlers

▲▽▲▽▲▽▲▽▲▽▲▽▲▽▲▽▲▽▲▽▲▽▲▽▲▽▲▽▲▽▲

BOARD BOOKS

CARROT SEED BOARD BOOK. (1993). Ruth Krauss. Illustrated by Crockett Johnson. New York: HarperCollins Children's Books. A small boy plants his very own carrot seed. Everyone tells him it won't grow, but he knows better.

THE FOUR SEASONS: AUTUMN, SPRING, SUMMER, WINTER. (1994). Gerda Muller. Edinburgh, Scotland: Floris Books. These four simple wordless books will lead the young child through the seasons of the year.

BOOKS

ALL ABOUT YOU. (1992). Catherine and Laurence Anholt. New York: Viking Children's Books. Cheerful pictures and gentle rhyming text invite very young children to think and talk about themselves and their world, from good morning and good night rituals to favorite foods, animals and toys.

BROWN BEAR, BROWN BEAR, WHAT DO YOU SEE? (1992). Bill Martin, Jr. Illustrated by Eric Carle. New York: Henry Holt and Company, Inc. An excellent beginning book of colors, with large double page illustrations of one animal asking another, "What do you see?" Young children delight in this kind of repetitive question and answer story.

COLORS EVERYWHERE. (1995). Tana Hoban. New York: Greenwillow Books. Tana Hoban looks at the riot of colors that surround us and makes us see them in different ways. She heightens our awareness and our vision, and the world will never look the same again. Exquisite photographs.

DADDIES. (1991). Adele A. Greenspun. New York: The Putnam Publishing Group. Beautiful black and white photographs depict the many special things that fathers can do with their children. The lyrical text complements each photograph.

FRIENDS IN THE PARK. (1993). Rochelle Bunnett. Illustrated by Carl Sahlhoff. New York: Checkerboard Press, Inc. Warm and sensitive text is paired with wonderful photographs. A group of young children of all abilities spends a day together in the park.

GOLDEN BEAR. (1992). Ruth Young. Illustrated by Rachel Isadora. New York: Viking Children's Books. Caldecott award-winning Rachel Isadora has created vivid illustrations to accompany this rhythmic story about a little boy and his perfect companion, Golden Bear.

HOP JUMP. (1993). Ellen S. Walsh. San Diego, CA: Harcourt Brace and Company. Hop Jump. Hop Jump. That's all the frogs can do until Betsy teaches them how to turn and twist like the leaves.

IN THE TALL, TALL GRASS. (1995). Denise Fleming. New York: Henry Holt and Company, Inc. Ms. Fleming illustrates this nature story with bold colorful pictures she creates by pouring cotton pulp through stenciled images. The image becomes part of the paper itself.

▲▽▲▽▲▽▲▽▲▽▲▽▲▽▲▽▲▽▲▽▲▽▲▽▲▽▲▽▲▽▲

LITTLE ELEPHANT. (1994). Miela Ford. Photographed by Tana Hoban. New York: Greenwillow Books. This is a gem of a photographic story for young children. The story is about a young elephant's adventures in the water, close to his mother.

NO NAP. (1989). Eve Bunting. New York: Houghton Mifflin Company. It's Susie's nap time, but Susie isn't tired. "No nap," she says. So Dad makes his own plans to tire Susie out. A fresh and humorous approach to a real life situation.

ON MOTHER'S LAP. (1992). Ann H. Scott. Illustrated by Glo Coalson. New York: Houghton Mifflin Company. Michael's favorite place to be is on Mother's lap, where there is room for all, including baby sister.

PIGGIES. (1994). Audrey Wood. San Diego, CA: Harcourt Brace and Company. Ten little piggies dance on a child's fingers and toes, doing the most amazing things until it's time for two wee kisses good night.

PRETEND YOURE A CAT. (1990). Jean Marzollo. Illustrated by Jerry Pinkney. New York: Dial Books for Young Readers. Caldecott Honor winner Jerry Pinkney has enhanced Jean Marzollo's exuberant verses in a way that stimulates the eye and the imagination. Even the shyest child will respond with enthusiasm to these rhymes.

SHEEP IN A JEEP. (1991). Nancy Shaw. Illustrated by Margot Apple. New York: Houghton Mifflin Company. Here is a lively funny tale, perfect for reading aloud. The youngest lap sitters will quickly learn to chant along with the reader.

SKA-TAT. (1993). Kimberly Knutson. New York: Macmillan Children Book Group. All around, twig-snappy piles and leaf mountains make interesting sounds. Jump into the fun of a crisp autumn day!

SLEEPY BEAR. (1993). Lydia Dabcovich. New York: Dutton Children's Books. The striking pictures carry children through fall, winter, spring and summer in a very realistic way.

SO MUCH. (1994). Trish Cooke. Illustrated by Helen Oxenbury. Cambridge, MA: Candlewick Press. Everybody wants to hug the baby, kiss the baby, squeeze the baby because they love him so much! Helen Oxenbury's illustrations capture the joy of being part of an extended family.

SUN, SNOW, STARS, SKY. (1995). Catherine Anholt. New York: Viking Children's Books. Cheery watercolor pictures and simple questions about the weather invite children to think and talk about the world around them.

WE'RE GOING ON A BEAR HUNT. (1989). Michael Rosen. Illustrated by Helen Oxenbury. New York: Macmillan Children's Book Group. An irresistible story, told in rhyme, full of fun and suspense, in which a father, four children and a dog set out on an unlikely family outing—a bear hunt.

WHAT IS THE SUN? (1994). Reeve Lindbergh. Illustrated by Stephen Lambert. Cambridge, MA: Candlewick Press. As a grandmother tucks her grandson in, she soothes his wondering mind with answers to his every question. He asks about the sun, the moon, stars, the wind, sea and rain.

Index

▲▼▲▼▲▼▲▼▲▼▲▼▲▼▲▼▲▼▲▼▲▼▲▼▲▼▲▼▲

▲▼▲▼▲▼▲▼▲▼▲▼▲▼▲▼▲▼▲▼▲▼▲▼▲▼▲

index ▲